The Catholic Guide to Loneliness

Other books by Kevin Vost
from Sophia Institute Press:

Memorize the Faith!

Fit for Eternal Life!

The One-Minute Aquinas

Unearthing Your Ten Talents

The Seven Deadly Sins

Hounds of the Lord

The Seven Gifts of the Holy Spirit

Kevin Vost, Psy.D.

The
CATHOLIC
GUIDE
—— TO ——
LONELINESS

*How Science and Faith
Can Help Us Understand It,
Grow from It, and Conquer It*

SOPHIA INSTITUTE PRESS
Manchester, New Hampshire

Sophia Institute Press
Box 5284, Manchester, NH 03108
1-800-888-9344

www.SophiaInstitute.com

Sophia Institute Press® is a registered trademark of Sophia Institute.

Library of Congress Cataloging-in-Publication Data

Names: Vost, Kevin, author.
Title: The Catholic guide to loneliness : how science and faith can help us understand it, grow from it, and conquer it / Kevin Vost, Psy.D.
Description: Manchester, New Hampshire : Sophia Institute Press, 2017. | Includes bibliographical references.
Identifiers: LCCN 2017030001 | ISBN 9781622824144 (pbk. : alk. paper)
Subjects: LCSH: Loneliness—Religious aspects—Catholic Church.
Classification: LCC BV4911 .V67 2017 | DDC 155.9/2—dc23 LC record available at https://lccn.loc.gov/2017030001

First printing

*To all who are lonely and all who reach out
to lighten the load of their neighbor's loneliness*

Contents

The Catholic Guide to Loneliness

Chapter 1

Rethinking and Relieving Loneliness

When I was a child, I spoke like a child. I reasoned like a child. When I became a man, I gave up childish ways.... Brethren, do not be children in your thinking; be babes in evil, but in thinking be mature.

—1 Corinthians 13:11; 14:20

Grown-Up Thinking about Loneliness

Loneliness is a product of our God-given human capacity to think and reflect about things. It is defined as a "perceived social isolation." Note the importance of the word *perceived*. We feel lonely when we think there is a discrepancy between the social connectedness we would like to have and that which we do have. This is not to say that loneliness is "all in one's head," something to be dismissed or ignored, since the lonely person's perception of a serious lack in social connection may be very accurate indeed. A quarter of the adults queried in a 2004 study reported that they had *no one* to confide in about serious matters. So, if you or I are feeling lonely, this may in no way imply that we are engaging in the kind of childish thinking that St. Paul has warned about. There may be many valid reasons for us to feel lonely, but what may be childish, or at least inaccurate, distressing, and self-defeating, in our thinking is how we proceed to think about the fact of our loneliness.

There could be a literally childish component to our thinking if our current experience of loneliness harks back to parental bonding and attachment difficulties in early childhood or perhaps to a sense of rejection from peers or even bullying later on. Still, as cognitive psychotherapists would start to argue in the 1950s and 1960s, and continue to argue, even when some childhood experiences seem to be causing us emotional distress as adults, the reason these experiences have the power to do so is because of how we think and talk to ourselves about those events *today*.

The ways we are accustomed to thinking about and talking to ourselves about negative events in our lives will determine, to a great extent, how much those events—even the kinds of personal loss or isolation that may leave us prey to loneliness—distress or immobilize us. To think like an adult about the experience of loneliness, we must ask ourselves, "Okay, so I'm lonely, now what am I going to do about it?" Well, I'm glad you asked yourself, since that's exactly what the rest of this book is about!

The ABCs of Lonely Thinking

"Maladaptive social cognition" refers to the kinds of thinking about social situations that tend to produce distress and make people less able to act in appropriate ways that can encourage engagement and connection with others.

Consider this hypothetical incident relevant to loneliness.[1] Let's say you see your friend Sally strolling by on the other side of the street. She looks your way, you wave exuberantly, and she continues on her way without a wave or even a smile. What do you do? Perhaps you deftly transform your wave to look as if you were just patting down your hair, as you hope that no one else

---

[1] Example adapted from Albert Ellis, Ph.D., and Robert Lange, Ed.D, *How to Keep People from Pushing Your Buttons* (Secaucus, NJ: Carol Publishing Group, 1994).

noticed the slight.[2] How do you feel? Embarrassed perhaps and saddened that you have been shunned? There is nothing unusual here, and it would seem to illustrate clearly a simple stimulus-response psychology. The stimulus (Sally's snub) has triggered your emotional response (embarrassment, sadness, perhaps even anger at Sally, and a sense of rejection and loneliness as well). Still, was it as simple as that?

Are we really black boxes, as many behaviorists suppose? *Important things go on inside an organism between a stimulus and a response.* In animals this would be instinct. In humans the intervening factor would be our abilities to think, to evaluate, and to talk to ourselves about the various stimuli we encounter through events in the world. After all, not every person reacts the same way to the same events.

In the world of psychotherapy, the greater awareness of the power of human thought or cognition gave rise in the 1960s to "cognitive therapy," which holds, for example, that a key component of depression is the way depressed people bring and keep themselves down by consistently thinking in negative ways about *their selves, the world,* and *the future.* By ferreting out and changing such patterns of thinking, depression can sometimes be quite successfully treated.

Shortly before this, in the mid-1950s, psychologist Albert Ellis had pioneered his Rational Therapy, later to be called Rational-Emotive Behavior Therapy (REBT). His most popular and influential early books on the subject included *A Guide to Rational Living,* first published in 1961, and *Reason and Emotion in Psychotherapy* in

---

[2] Ever done such a thing yourself? These almost reflexive kinds of transformations of movements to avoid embarrassment are called "modifiers" in the language of body language studies.

1962. In the early 1960s, Ellis applied his theories to all kinds of mental disorders and emotional distresses. He boiled down countless problems to their simple ABCs.

Let S (the stimulus) be A (an *activating event*), and let R (the response) be C (the emotional/behavioral *consequence*).

Stimulus = Actuating event
Response = Consequence (emotional/behavioral)

When Sally passes by (A) and we are embarrassed or sad or angry (C), we tend to act as if A caused C—but Ellis points out the often-neglected but most important causal factor. Let the activities of the organism (O) be represented here by B (our *beliefs*).

Stimulus = Actuating event
Us = Beliefs
Response = Consequence (emotional/behavioral)

Sally did not cause us to feel a certain way. We caused those feelings ourselves!

How can we show this? Let's say, for example, that as you walk on, all disgruntled, you see Sally getting out of her car on your side of the street, and she beams you a smile and calls you over. Oops! That person you had waved to wasn't Sally after all. Are you still sad or mad at her?

Or let's say it was Sally. You see her later, and she tells you that she just got back from the eye doctor and her pupils were dilated, or she wasn't wearing her contacts, or she just heard some tragic news and was lost in thought. Are you still sad or mad? Let's hope not!

This is one simple way we can see how our beliefs or cognitive evaluations determine our emotional reactions. Methods that Albert Ellis and other cognitive therapists employ train us to examine the accuracy of our thinking in social situations, since our habitual initial reactions in the form of "automatic thoughts" serve to distress us without our full conscious awareness. Adapting such methods to question our first impressions of potentially distressing situations we encounter can go a long way toward alleviating all kinds of emotional distress, including loneliness.

But Ellis's ABC system of psychotherapy goes much deeper even than this. He not only advises us to make sure that our beliefs (Bs) accurately reflect activating events (As). *What if Sally did snub us?* Must we still become embarrassed, sad, angry, or lonely? More accurately stated, must we still *make ourselves* embarrassed, sad, angry, or lonely? Ellis answers with an emphatic *no!*

If we became embarrassed, sad, or angry only when we suffered true injustices of various sorts — well, as fallible and sinful creatures, we would still go around embarrassed, sad, angry, or lonely a good deal of the time! Further, Ellis notes that when we suffer various slights or ills, insults or injuries, we tend to keep ruminating about the incidents, stacking one irrational belief upon another as we talk to ourselves about them. If we feel slighted, we might start questioning our own worth: *Hmmm, didn't Sally also slight me last week?* If we feel angry, we might start cataloging Sally's other faults and work ourselves up against her. We might even realize at some point that we are being a bit unreasonable and then start to bash ourselves for it: *Oh, I always overreact! What a sad specimen am I!*

Ellis states that many irrational and self-harming beliefs are common to humanity. He is known for creating a list of 11 common irrational beliefs but once noted that he came up with a much fuller list of 259! I will mention here only his first one for its special relevance to the experience of loneliness:

Irrational Belief #1: "It is a dire necessity for adult human beings to be loved or approved of by virtually every significant other person in their community."

According to Ellis, people tend to hold this unrealistic belief and to upset themselves needlessly again and again when their expectation is not met and they suffer any kind of rejection from others. A recent research study has shown that the experience of feeling one has been snubbed, even during an experiment, can have real consequences, firing up activity in one's dorsal anterior cingulate cortex, the same brain center that lights up in response to pain.[3] There is more to loneliness than having been snubbed, but the same cognitive principles apply to many situations associated with loneliness.[4]

So how can we employ this "ABC model" to help ourselves cope with snubbing and with all kinds of situations that might

---

[3] John T. Cacioppo and William Patrick, *Loneliness: Human Nature and the Need for Social Connection* (New York: W. W. Norton, 2008), 9.

[4] I should make readers aware that Ellis, an atheist, believed that religions, including Christianity, actually promote these kinds of irrational beliefs. Still, I would opine that regarding Irrational Belief #1, if we tell ourselves that everyone must love us, we haven't picked that up from the Scriptures or the Church. Jesus told us that those who follow Him may well face persecution, rather than love, from their neighbors. We are commanded to love our neighbor, with no guarantee that our neighbor will love us in return. Christ's Church, after all, was built by martyrs, and His own death was the first. To Ellis's credit, though, when later scientific research made clear that religious beliefs often help people mentally and emotionally, he was willing to coauthor a book on using Rational Emotive Behavior Therapy with religious clients.

lead to all varieties of emotional distress, including that which comes with loneliness? Well, this is where *D* and *E* come into play. When we experience a slight or insult that leads us to feeling upset, we need to become aware of our *B*s — our beliefs — the kinds of things we are thinking and repeating to ourselves that make us upset. Then we need to bring in the *D*, that is, to *dispute* those beliefs, to make ourselves aware of their irrationality and replace them with saner ways of looking at the situation. When we have done so successfully, then *E*, the new emotional consequence, will take its place as we become less distressed and better able to get on with our lives. (On the next page, I've laid this out succinctly for the worst of the two Sally scenarios, the one in which she has really snubbed us.)

When I Know My ABCs, It Won't Matter What You Think of Me

This method for treating a variety of problems, including the distress of loneliness, is at its core nothing new. Stoic philosophers of two millennia ago emphasized that our enduring emotions and behaviors are determined more by our own thinking than by external events. Indeed, the most direct statement of this idea is found in the writings of Epictetus (55–135), a philosopher and former slave (indeed, his very name in Greek comes from a word meaning "acquired").

Epictetus was a master of philosophical psychology and a staunch advocate of living a life of virtue, above all by following the will of God. He presented the core of what would become cognitive therapy millennia later most clearly and succinctly in his *Enchiridion* (*Handbook*): "What upsets people is not things

The ABCs of Emotional

Activating Event	Beliefs (Irrational)	Consequence (Emotional)
Sally snubs us.	"Other people saw her snub me. They think I must not be important to her."	Embarrassment
	"I don't rate with her. How terrible!"	Sadness
	"How dare she! How wicked!"	Anger

themselves but their judgments about the things."[5] His philosophy focused largely on training people to distinguish between the things they can control and the things they cannot control, and then to waste no time in disturbing themselves over things they cannot control, which include the behaviors of other people. The key things within our control are our thought processes, judgments, and "moral purpose," that is, our abilities to regulate our emotions and guide our behaviors by what is true and right, regardless of external circumstances.

Early Christians such as Origen and St. John Chrysostom were among many prominent Catholic thinkers who acknowledged

[5] *The Handbook of Epictetus*, ed. Nicholas P. White (Indianapolis, IN: Hackett, 1983), 13.

Disturbance (and Healing)

Disputation of Beliefs	Emotional Consequence (New One)
"This can happen to anyone and others don't really understand the situation. I won't sweat it."	At most, very mild chagrin
"That's her opinion! So what!"	Mild disappointment
"That's her problem. I'll pray for her."	Mild irritation, and concern for Sally

Epictetus's practical wisdom. Many centuries later in the 1200s, St. Thomas Aquinas, when expounding upon the nature of man in his masterful *Summa Theologica*, would draw openly from the writings of Lucius Annaeus Seneca (4 B.C.–A.D. 65), a Latin-writing Stoic whose fundamental ideas on reason as a regulator of emotion echoed those of Epictetus.

Modern psychology and psychiatry were many centuries behind the curve of Catholic wisdom in this regard, and I'll draw from such wisdom in our very next chapter. But in recent decades therapists have certainly made the most of the fact that there are ways in which we can train ourselves to think rationally about all sorts of external events, including those that promote loneliness, that can drastically lessen their capacities to distress and incapacitate us.

Why and How You Should Hone Your Social Thinking Skills

One approach to loneliness that can benefit some people is training in *social skills*, such as how to make eye contact, start conversations, ask questions of others, and so forth. These skills are indeed quite valuable to initiating and sustaining meaningful interpersonal interactions, but research has shown that most lonely adults *already possess such skills*. Rather, it is the kind of *distorted thinking* that we are all prone to — and that loneliness can make worse — that can *keep people from using the skills they possess*. Yes, you've got it: "maladaptive social cognition" is at it again.

Loneliness can have an adaptive value like that of physical pain, acting as an alarm that something is amiss when a person becomes lonely through no direct choice of his own. Be it from the loss of a loved one through death or divorce, relocating away from friends and family for a job or for school, or whatever the reason, this sense of isolation will prompt a person to try to reconnect and make things right again. The distress that accompanies severe loneliness, however, can sometimes disturb one's thinking about how to interconnect by making one hyperalert to possible social threats or rejections. For example, lonely people may become more likely to interpret another person's behavior toward them as implying rejection, when such is not the case. In this hypersensitive state, the lonely person can also develop biases in thinking, focusing on and remembering negative social interactions and experiences, while ignoring or making light of positive ones. In some people this can lead to paranoid or aggressive behaviors as they come to expect that others will reject them. This, in turn, can lead the lonely, without their awareness, to alter, abate, or turn off their social skills, perhaps not risking a smile or a greeting or extending or accepting an invitation. It can also set up a "self-fulfilling prophecy" when people, expecting to be rejected, act in the kinds of overly passive, aggressive, paranoid, or pessimistic ways that make actual rejection more likely.

Methods of cognitive therapies can help lonely people identify these tendencies in themselves and try to circumvent them, and I must admit that I've used them myself. Allow me to elaborate.

Various cognitive therapists have cataloged a slew of automatic tendencies in human thinking that can cause us unnecessarily to upset ourselves, especially in social situations. One of the most important is that of "awfulizing" or "catastrophizing," the tendency to make mountains out of molehills, making situations out to be worse than they are or might become. Let me use the example of public speaking, the fear of which is very common among the general public.[6] Perhaps you have experienced it yourself.

We might think it would be awful if we gave a speech poorly before a crowd. Cognitive therapists would advise us to give it our best shot and to tell ourselves beforehand that it would be only mildly unfortunate and certainly not awful if we failed.

Here are a couple of ways you could apply this. Let's say you have to give a speech. Relax, and imagine this scene, if you will: you stand in a crowded room, mumble and mispronounce your first words, crack a joke that meets with silence, knock over your glass of water, realize that you've accidentally spit on the folks

---

[6] Indeed, there are many recent research articles in psychiatry and psychology journals on the subject. I just did a quick Internet search, and one that caught my eye was about the problem of public-speaking anxiety even among students in medical schools.

in the first row, and when you look down, you notice that your shoes don't match—and your zipper is down. Try to imagine this scene vividly and to imagine saying something like this to yourself: "Oh well, nobody's perfect! That would not be fun, but it wouldn't be awful either. I would not be the world's greatest public speaker. I might even be the worst, but somebody's gotta be, I suppose, and life would still go on."

No, that scenario did not actually happen to me, but it illustrates that if we can train ourselves to cope mentally with even big problems that probably won't ever arise, we'll be much better able to handle the lesser problems that may well come to pass during a presentation.[7]

Now, here is my own story of public-speaking anxiety. Being of a rather high-strung, sensitive, and nervous temperament (in short, shy), when I was young and had to speak in public, my body would rebel against me (technical term—"excessive physiological activity") by making my face flush, my voice falter, and my heart pound. Of course, I would fear that people would notice these things (which, of course, they did). This was so severe that, while wishing no harm to my teacher, I would sometimes speculate on the odds that he or she would get ill before the end of the term so I would not have to give the talk! Indeed, some of my family members were shocked when I later became a college professor and a public speaker!

The last presentation that I faced with such fear, trepidation, and bodily rebellion was during my junior year in college, the year in which I began to study cognitive psychotherapy. When

---

[7] I sometimes wonder if anyone who has used electronic audio-visual aids in his talks has ever given a talk without some kind of computerized glitch!

I got up in front of my professor and my classmates, I simply asked aloud that everyone bear with me if they could see my heart pounding in my chest, and I got on with it. I have never felt awful about the prospect of a speech again and have never again had to start a talk with such a warning.

I chose to make the supposedly horrible consequence happen—that people would notice that I was really nervous—and in doing so, I realized that it really was no big deal. Ever since that experience, I have focused on my subject matter and not on what people might think about me, and what a difference that makes!

I relate my story in the hope that once you see that you can learn adaptive social thinking, training yourself to think more calmly and rationally in very intense social situations such as giving a speech, you will certainly be able to do so in less stressful one-on-one interactions that might well lead to new connections and the dispelling of loneliness. Indeed, Albert Ellis himself wrote that he first realized the value of rational thinking methods like the ones he had learned from Epictetus when he found that they enabled him as a young man to muster up the courage to talk to young women!

Three Remedies for Loneliness through Training

So then, here are three important ways in which training in more rational thinking about social situations, either through self-study and practice or with a cognitive therapist, if necessary, can help you overcome or at least better cope with loneliness.

First, adaptive social thinking can help you better apply the people skills you probably already have in connecting with new people, especially if you are rusty or if prolonged loneliness, or the events that led to it, have distorted your thinking, making you more suspicious of others or hypersensitive to possible criticism or rejection. Indeed, you can work to inoculate yourself by preparing in advance for such situations.

The Stoic philosopher and Roman emperor Marcus Aurelius (121–180) gave noble advice we can use to brace ourselves for all manner of responses we may receive from others if we try to reach out to them. He advised that every morning on arising, we should remind ourselves that we are going to encounter "the busybody, the thankless, the overbearing, the treacherous, the envious, the unneighborly,"[8] which surely rings as true in our day as it did in the second century. Aurelius elaborated that some people act this way because they do not truly understand good and evil, and that we should not be debased or discouraged by *their* actions.

Further, if our own social thinking is on the mark, we will recall that these people share the same humanity with us, and we must still value them as kinsmen, placed in the world for cooperation, and not for resentment or avoidance. Such thinking can reduce our tendencies to react with anger toward others and to be hypersensitive to how others might react unfairly to our kindly overtures, intended to establish or nourish connections. If we can anticipate in advance that our friendly gestures might not be reciprocated as we hope, and accept it, we can better muster the courage to reach out anyway.

Second, more adaptive social thinking can help us combat the self-destructive behaviors that sometimes accompany loneliness. The problem of loneliness is so perennial and pervasive that it can show

---

[8] Marcus Aurelius, *Meditations* (Cambridge, MA: Harvard University Press), 305.

its face in some of the most surprising places. In rereading *How to Lower Your Fat Thermostat*, one of my favorite fitness and nutrition books, written by a physician, a physiologist, and a psychologist, I rediscovered that psychologist Edward Parent had included an entire section on how loneliness can lead to overeating as a means of self-comfort. If done excessively, it can lead to the kind of weight gain that makes the lonely feel more ashamed and even less likely to try to reconnect with others. While Parent mentions the value of common remedies for loneliness, such as joining a church group or other social groups and even acquiring a pet (all the better if one can walk it outside and perhaps interact with one's neighbors), he too focused on training oneself in rational, appropriate thinking about social situations. Here is his example:

> If you look at your self-talk, it is likely that you are saying something like, "It is awful being alone all the time and I can't stand it. I have to get away from this terrible feeling." You can dispute these ideas with something like, "I prefer having fun companions with whom to share my life. However, rather than feeling sorry for myself, I will work on making myself the most attractive and interesting person I can be. This will maximize my chances of finding an acceptable companion but, more importantly, will help me to be better company when I am alone."[9]

You will recognize in Parent's practical recommendations some of the adaptive social-thinking techniques we looked at previously,

---

[9] Dennis Remington, M.D., Garth Fisher, Ph.D., and Edward Parent, Ph.D., *How to Lower Your Fat Thermostat: The No-Diet Reprogramming Plan for Lifelong Weight Control* (Provo, UT: Vitality House, 1983), 171.

such as the causal power of how we talk to ourselves, the need to combat "awfulizing" tendencies, and the need rationally to dispute such maladaptive ways of thinking. The same methods can be used to attack other self-destructive behaviors that might accompany feelings of loneliness, such as excessive use of alcohol, smoking, or avoidance of exercise.

As Catholics, we would also do well to consider that we will engage in fewer self-destructive behaviors when we seriously ponder and take heed of St. Paul's words that our bodies are temples of the Holy Spirit (1 Cor. 6:19). Further, we will be truly most "attractive and interesting" when we most fully imitate and join with Christ and say to ourselves, as St. Paul did: "I have been crucified with Christ; it is no longer I who live, but Christ who lives in me: and the life I now live in the flesh I live by faith in the Son of God, who loved me and gave himself for me" (Gal. 2:20).

Third, more adaptive social thinking can help us better bear the cross of loneliness if it persists, realizing that, although unpleasant, it is not awful, will not last forever, and can be borne for as long as necessary. As Catholics, we are all for human reason and the benefits it can bring, but we acknowledge as well the "wisdom from above" (James 3:17), whereby God Himself can give us the grace and the strength we need to bear with and overcome any adversity we may face, including the face of loneliness. Indeed, St. James tells us that we should "count it all joy" when we "meet various trials," because "the testing of [our] faith produces steadfastness" (James 1:2–3).

In our next chapter, we'll dig deep into the treasury of Catholic wisdom from above that we can glean from the Church's most profound thinkers about the human condition. We'll see how the trials and tribulations of life, even those of loneliness, can help make us grow more steadfast in our faith—and ultimately lead us to deeper joy on earth and the eternal and unfathomable joy of emotional and social connections with the community of saints in heaven, as we share in the beatific vision of the glorious God, who created and connected us all.

Action Plan

Read. Epictetus's *Enchiridion* or *Handbook* is a very brief summary of his philosophy in fifty-three short paragraphs. It provides many simple, yet profound lessons that can be read and reread to help calm oneself and learn to cope better with all sorts of emotional distresses, including the pains of loneliness. Although this first-century philosopher was not a Christian himself and did not appear to be very conversant with this then-new religion, in later centuries many Catholic thinkers found so many useful insights in the *Handbook* that they adapted it for use by monks in monasteries. Indeed, three "Christianized" adaptations (which, for example, substituted the name of St. Paul for Socrates, or which compared Epictetus's lessons to the lessons in particular scriptural passages) were prepared from the fifth to the fourteenth centuries. One version, known as the *Vaticanus graecus* edition, was found housed in the library of the Vatican.[10] For another text much closer to the Catholic Faith that can help realign your thinking about the things that really matter, I recommend

---

[10] It is quite a scholarly text, but I'll note for interested readers that the story is told and the manuscripts are provided in Gerard Boter's *Enchiridion of Epictetus and Its Three Christian Adaptations* (Boston: Brill, 1999).

a rereading of Jesus Christ's Sermon on the Mount in chapters 5, 6, and 7 of Matthew's Gospel.

Reflect. The core message of this chapter is the need to improve our ability to reflect, to think deeply and appropriately about the kinds of social situations, rejections, or losses that may lead us to feelings of loneliness, so that by thinking in healthier ways we might feel less distressed.

The next time you feel lonely, see if you can catch your own Bs — the beliefs, automatic thoughts, or things that you've said to yourself that have prompted your distress. Were your thoughts accurate and realistic? Were they adaptive, helpful to you in some way, or did they serve only to bring you down? Can you take out a piece of paper and write down, or sit at your keyboard and type out, the ABCs of the situation? Can you then complete the *D* and *E*? — that is, dispute the particular thoughts that brought you down and come up with a less distressing new emotional consequence? If you can train yourself to go through this process for actual events, emotions, and thoughts in your life, you may find that eventually your automatic thoughts will become far less distressing and immobilizing, leaving you feeling less lonely and better able to get out and do something about it.

Remember. Honestly consider whether you have been selective in your memories of social interactions, recalling only the losses, rejections, or failures while ignoring the many ways in which God has blessed you in relationships with others. If you have, do something about it. Purposefully recall and enjoy those positive past events and motivate yourself to create some new ones.

Recite. There is nothing at all wrong with asking God to help you improve your social cognition, your ability to think about social situations in a way that will lesson your loneliness. St. Thomas Aquinas had a formal prayer for God's guidance in his thinking in his "Ante Studium" (Before Study). Here is a brief excerpt:

> *Ineffable Creator,*
> *Who, from the treasures of Your wisdom,*
> *have established three hierarchies of angels,*
> *have arrayed them in marvelous order*
> *above the fiery heavens,*
> *and have marshaled the regions*
> *of the universe with such artful skill . . .*
> *Grant to me keenness of mind,*
> *capacity to remember,*
> *skill in learning,*
> *subtlety to interpret,*
> *and eloquence of speech.*
> *May you guide the beginning of my work,*
> *direct its progress, and bring it to completion.*[11]

Can you craft your own brief prayer to request God's guidance in using the reasoning powers He gave you to cope with loneliness?

Reconnect. Can you think of a simple act to reach out to another person to lessen your loneliness or to lessen the other person's? If you can think of such an act but have not acted on it, can

---

[11] *The Aquinas Prayer Book: The Prayer and Hymns of St. Thomas Aquinas,* trans. and ed. Robert Anderson and Johann Moser (Manchester, NH: Sophia Institute Press, 2000), 43.

you pin down the thoughts that are holding you back, dispute them, and then go out and get the job done? Thoughts, emotions, and behaviors are closely intertwined, and sometimes if we are feeling down or our thoughts are in a rut, simply *acting* in some small way by reaching out to another can dislodge dammed-up thoughts and elevate depressed emotions.

The Survival (and Redemptive) Value of Loneliness

Loneliness hurts, but it can serve more than one useful purpose. On the purely human plane, modern researchers build upon evolutionary theory to assert that the human capacity to feel lonely is a very valuable one. They argue that *loneliness is the social equivalent of physical pain.* As physical pain protects us from bodily harm, so too may the *social pain* of loneliness protect an individual from the dangers that may accompany isolation from his group, his source of safety, and support. Just as a person who does not feel pain is at great risk of harm, so too would be a person who never felt lonely. With the extended helpless infancy of human beings, this need for social connection and pain is, in its absence, stronger among humans than among animals.[12]

---

[12] While modern researchers tend to flesh out their theories with an evolutionary perspective, I'll note that man's uniquely social nature has long been recognized by a variety of thinkers who examined human nature. Aristotle, for example, as we'll see in chapter 6, described human beings as not only unique as the only "rational animals" but also as the only "political animals." Although all kinds of animals have social bonds of various kinds, only human beings form *poleis* (cities) and govern themselves by means of their intellects and wills.

In essence then, even in adulthood, feelings of loneliness may serve a valuable service if they motivate us to connect or reconnect on the personal, relational, or collective level. Loneliness has been compared to the physical sensation of thirst as well as to pain. Loneliness may well be painful, but how dangerous or at least empty life would be if we did not even care if we had become isolated from others and had no thirst to reconnect.

Further, from the Catholic perspective, the experience of loneliness may bring with it at times even deeper and more lasting value. It may open us up to a closer relationship with God as we offer up our emotional pain and embrace redemptive suffering through Christ. It may also enhance our awareness and motivate us to strive to help heal the loneliness of our neighbors, as we will see in the pages ahead.

Chapter 2

The Virtues of Loneliness

Since happiness is the perfect and sufficient good, it must
needs set man's desire at rest and exclude every evil....
Wherefore also according to the Philosopher (*Ethics*, 1:9), happiness is the reward of works of virtue.

—St. Thomas Aquinas, *Summa Theologica*, I-II, Q. 5. arts. 4, 5

Now I wish to tell you further, that a man proves his
patience on his neighbor, when he receives injuries from
him. Similarly, he proves his humility on a proud man,
his faith on an infidel, his true hope one who despairs,
his justice on the unjust, his kindness on the cruel, his
gentleness and benignity on the irascible. Good men produce and prove all their virtues on their neighbor....

—St. Catherine of Siena, *Dialogue*

You Have Been Crafted for Earthly and Eternal Happiness

Prolonged, severe loneliness can be distressing, with negative impacts on mental and physical health. Perceived lack of intimacy and belonging is clearly a threat to our happiness and, indeed, is a real evil when evil is understood as a lack of a good that should be present. God made us to connect and share with each other. We have seen that by changing the ways we talk to ourselves about situations that might prompt feelings of loneliness we can alleviate some of the unhappiness that loneliness can usher in. Still, God does not want us to merely be less unhappy. As St. Irenaeus stated so well eighteen centuries ago, "The glory of God is man fully alive, and the life of man is the vision of God."[13] One hundred years before Irenaeus's birth, God made Himself visible and explained in His own words why He came to the people on earth: "I came that they may have life, and have it abundantly" (John 10:10).

---

[13] Irenaeus, *Against Heresies*, IV, 20, 7, as cited in Mons. Phillipe Delhaye, *Pope John Paul II on the Contemporary Importance of St. Irenaeus*, no. 10, http://www.ewtn.com/library/theology/irenaeus.htm.

St. Thomas Aquinas added that God intends for us a *twofold happiness*: an *imperfect* happiness while here on earth and a *perfect* happiness in heaven. Starting with Aristotle and concluding with St. Matthew, Thomas tells us: "The Philosopher, in placing man's happiness in this life (*Ethics*, 1:10), says it is imperfect, and after a long discussion concludes: We call men happy, but only as men. But God has promised us perfect happiness, when we shall be as the angels ... in heaven (Matt. 22:30)."[14]

And what are the keys to both kinds of happiness?

We saw in this chapter's first quotation that St. Thomas Aquinas claims that *virtues* hold the keys to happiness. Virtues are habits or dispositions to know the truth and to do the good. They perfect our powers as human beings made in the image and likeness of God with intellects and wills. They perfect the capacities of our intellects to know what is true, and the capacities of our wills to rein in our passions and desires to keep us from doing what is wrong and to guide us toward what is right. The more we embrace and build these capacities, the happier we become and the less susceptible to negative attitudes and emotions, including those that accompany excessive, prolonged loneliness.

Now, there are important *natural virtues*, such as temperance, fortitude, justice, and prudence, long known to great pagan philosophers. And literally thanks be to God, there are also *supernatural, theological,* or *infused virtues* that the Father and the Son freely bestow on us through the workings of the Holy Spirit: faith, hope, and love (also called charity). All the virtues work together to guide us toward that imperfect happiness we can experience on earth and the perfect eternal bliss we hope to share: the beatific vision of God in heaven.

---

[14] *Summa Theologica* (*ST*), I-II, Q. 3, art. 2.

So how do we build these virtues, and how can they alleviate loneliness? Those are the questions to which we'll now turn.

How to Acquire the Virtues
That Can Conquer Loneliness

What must we do to build in ourselves the kinds of virtues that can help us cope with and overcome loneliness? As for virtue building in general, Aristotle astutely observed 2,300 years ago that "we become builders by building and harpists by playing the harp." His observation still holds true to this day — and not just for builders and harpists! Virtues are built through repeated practice. Practice makes perfect virtues, we might say.

Of course, this implies that we have some capacity for the virtues in us already, or we would not even be able to start practicing them. Recall that virtues perfect our intellects and our wills. God has given us all the ability to think and to choose. When we train ourselves to think and choose well repeatedly, these acts become *habits, firm dispositions*, so that future virtuous acts become all the easier, and nearly automatic, becoming, well, habitual.

To draw a parallel with the last chapter's lessons from cognitive psychotherapy, a person who has trained himself in a virtue will have intentionally trained himself in appropriate, adaptive, ethical, happiness-promoting automatic thoughts when encountering challenging situations that call forth that virtue.

In a moment, we will consider particular virtues and particular situations relating to loneliness. First, let me comment on our opening quotation from one of the treatises in St. Catherine of Siena's *Dialogue*, during which God spoke directly to her in mystical ecstasy. The words in our quotation, then, come from God.

Note in His comments on virtues that they are built by encountering problems and challenges, especially social ones, arising from our interactions with each other. Ironically perhaps, it is often the follies and foibles of our loved ones and neighbors that provide the trials and tribulations, the testing grounds for our own growth in virtue as we react with virtuous thoughts, emotions, and deeds to their perhaps less than virtuous testing. We build patience when we interact with people who try our patience. So, too, may we be in the best position to build a panoply of virtues that can help us counter loneliness when we've been stung by rejection from others or suffered some kind of serious interpersonal loss that gives rise to our sense of emotional or social isolation. Let's see, then, how this works for a number of core virtues and a multitude of their allied virtues.

How to Connect with Others through the Cardinal Virtues

The four cardinal virtues of temperance, fortitude, justice, and prudence have been praised in the writings of pagan philosophers, in Scripture, and by modern psychologists.[15] They are known as

[15] Appearing as *andreia, sophrosyne, phronesis,* and *diakaiosyne* in Greek in the writings of Plato, Aristotle, Musonius Rufus, and many others; praised and cited together in the Old Testament, as in Wisdom 8:7: "And if anyone loves righteousness, her labors are virtues: for she teaches self-control and prudence, justice and courage; nothing in life is more profitable for men than these"; and endorsed for their psychological value by modern philosophers, theologians, and psychologists. See, for example, Romanus Cessario, O.P, Craig Steven Titus, and Paul Vitz, *Philosophical Virtues and Psychological Strengths* (Manchester, NH: Sophia Institute Press, 2013).

cardinal virtues from the Latin word *cardine*, "hinge," since all kinds of other virtues depend on, assist, or hinge on them, so to speak. In the pages ahead, we'll see plenty of examples of the way St. Thomas Aquinas made clear that a host of other virtues are required to express fully these cardinal four. They are called *moral* virtues because they perfect our moral actions toward ourselves and others, leading us away from the weakness, self-destruction, and harm to others that come from sins of commission or omission. Now let's dig right in to see how these spiritual excellences can help overcome the distress of loneliness.

Temperance
Temperance, moderation, or self-control is the virtue through which we rein in our sensual desires for things such as food, drink, and sexual activities: what St. Thomas called our "concupiscible appetites." Such desires are good in and of themselves, of course, for we must eat and drink to keep ourselves alive, and we must procreate, as God had commanded Adam and Eve, to "be fruitful and multiply, and fill the earth" (Gen. 1:28). The passions themselves, though, can wreak great havoc unless controlled by our God-given powers of reason. Too much or inappropriate food, drink, or sexual activity can lead to obesity, alcoholism, and all sorts of sexual ills. Intemperance is the source of many evils that plague us today, from diseases to ruined marriages, to a culture that promotes abortion.

Moreover, research has shown that, for some people, prolonged loneliness can increase the likelihood of excessive eating and drinking. Sometimes the profoundly lonely will also reach out to the wrong people or open themselves to potentially harmful sexual relationships to try to help alleviate their sense of emotional isolation, while oftentimes thereby increasing it. Clearly, temperance is well worth cultivating to help avoid some of the potentially self-destructive, loneliness-increasing behaviors that loneliness may usher in.

How can we grow in temperance? Recalling our lessons from the last chapter, *changing our thinking* about our excessive sensual desires is one place to start. We can train ourselves to stop and reflect when, for example, we desire more food than we need, asking ourselves if we really need the next helping or treat, or if we are irrationally using food to compensate for our loneliness and if there are not more positive things we can do that might get at the root of the problem.

Of course, we also need to "walk our self-talk," so to speak. Remembering that virtues are built through practice and that the cardinal virtues have related or allied lesser virtues, we can note that temperance has a great helper in the virtue of *continence*. You are continent when you experience an internal struggle to indulge in some inappropriate sensual gratification, but you prevail and do not give in. Imagine you are home alone or at the office or some public place surrounded by others, but you are feeling pangs of loneliness and disconnection. A second helping or a second dessert might seem especially tempting, and lately you have not exactly been a paragon of dietary temperance. Still, if you feel sorely tempted, but you talk yourself through the temptation and decide to forgo that extra sweet you do not need, you have exercised continence. When such acts of continence are repeated over time, they can blossom into the full-blown virtue of temperance, whereby you are no longer even tempted, even if feeling lonely.

St. Thomas writes about another virtue that might not at first appear to relate to the virtue of temperance, let alone loneliness. But bear with me and I think you'll agree that it is even more relevant and valuable in our own day than it was in St. Thomas's time. This is the virtue of *studiositas* (studiousness), which opposes the vice of *curiositas* (curiosity).

Of course, there is a sense in which it is a very good thing to be curious and open to learning about important things, but the vice of curiosity implies a curiosity about things that really don't matter at the expense of things that do. Thomas notes that curiosity is derived from *cura* (care) and refers to caring about the wrong kind of things, citing St. Paul, "wherefore the Apostle says (Rom. 13:14): *Make no provision (curam) for the flesh in its concupiscences.*" St. Augustine called it "concupiscence of the eyes" since it is most frequently expressed through seeking things to look at.

The virtue of studiousness, on the contrary, refers to our ability to care about, focus on, and study deeply the kinds of things that do matter, such as matters of the Faith and matters of our neighbor's well-being.

Why do I argue that the vice of curiosity is rampant today, conducive to loneliness, and that we need the virtue of studiousness perhaps as never before? Well, our world has become one of increasing emotional and social isolation while, at least in the United States, children are diagnosed with attention deficit disorder in unheard of numbers, and some adults are, too. Truly, the twin technological marvels of television and the Internet (via computers and various "smart" devices) have opened us up to unbounded curiosity and fleeting attention like nothing experienced before in human history. As television progressed from a handful of channels that we had to get up off the couch to change, to hundreds of channels to "surf" from that couch with a point and a click of the finger, the Internet has provided us with as many sites to "surf" as there are waves in the seven seas!

Although I haven't the time or the space to dig into this too deeply, those who might like to practice the virtue of studiousness are directed to works such as Nicholas Carr's *The Shallows: What the Internet Is Doing to Our Brains.*[16] Carr argues that by repeatedly practicing the sweeping, but fleeting and superficial scanning of information that electronic formats on the Internet supply, we are actually producing changes in our brain tissues and organization that make prolonged, sustained attention more difficult.

Like that book's author (and this one's, for that matter), have you experienced greater difficulty, for example, in sitting down and reading one book for a considerable chunk of time, having become accustomed to the swift perusal of mere bits and pieces of information through Internet sites and articles, most of which tend to be very brief and rich in hyperlinks to lead you away to other brief snippets suffused throughout the Web? Might this self-training in scattered and shallow attention make you less attentive to the emotional and social needs of those around you? Could Web surfing's nearly addictive appeal (though occasionally you might come across something truly worthwhile) be stealing your time away from paying attention and forming and nourishing true bonds with the people around you? If so, you would do well to exercise your continence and build up your temperance to limit and moderate the time you spend on such electronic activities.

Fortitude

Fortitude is the virtue that enables us to overcome obstacles and endure difficulties in order to achieve what is truly good for us.

---

[16] Nicholas Carr, *The Shallows: What the Internet Is Doing to Our Brains* (New York: W. W. Norton, 2011).

The word comes from the Latin *fortis*, for "strength," and *courage* is a common synonym. It is fortitude that helps us "fight the good fight" (1 Tim. 6:12). St. Thomas explains that as temperance directs and controls the concupiscible appetite for what we desire, fortitude harnesses the *irascible* appetite, which raises our ire, so to speak, so that we can fight against obstacles that thwart our desires.

So how might the virtue of fortitude fortify us and help us take heart in the face of loneliness? For one thing, it can help us take the kinds of risks in reaching out to others that might put an end to our loneliness. Recall how the experience of loneliness may warp our thinking in various ways, leading us to "awfulize," for example, and fear the worst if we reached out and someone rejected us. By training ourselves to rethink such situations and refusing to awfulize, we can bolster the virtue of fortitude in ourselves by being brave enough to make those initial overtures to another person that might make all the difference.

Further, St. Thomas said that the primary act of fortitude is to endure hardships, and this is seen in the operation of the related virtues of *patience* and *perseverance*. These virtues will enable us to bear with rejection if we should be rejected and to keep on trying. Recall St. Catherine of Siena's lesson from God: "A man proves his patience with his neighbor, when he receives injury from him." (In case it does not go without saying, "man" here is used in the most general sense. It applies just as well to a woman, as I'm sure St. Catherine herself could attest!)

So then, if you are lonely and are trying to do something about it, consider both St. Catherine's and Marcus Aurelius's lessons. Prepare yourself in advance by imagining that a friendly overture you may be planning may well lead to rejection this time, but it is by such experiences that the patience of fortitude is "proved," built up in your soul to help you persevere and endure the experience of loneliness if it should last for some time.

Justice

Justice, says St. Thomas, boils down to giving others their "rightful due." The most fundamental precepts of justice are to "do the good" and "do not do evil." Now, if we all gave every person his rightful due, not only in terms of things such as the money we might owe them or the services or obligations we have promised to fulfill, but in terms of attention, respect, courtesy, friendliness, honesty, gratitude, and the like, there would surely be far less loneliness in the world. Indeed, many of these behaviors themselves sprout from the virtues that make justice complete. St. Thomas treats of *dulia* (respect), truthfulness, affability (friendliness), and gratitude as among the virtues that in themselves flesh out the virtue of justice we owe to one another. If we strive to develop these virtues by practicing them ourselves, we become less likely to prompt rejection from others, and, of course, if others still treat us unjustly, we can call on the virtue of patience in our souls.

In one of my favorite bits of practical advice from St. Thomas Aquinas, he builds upon the Stoic philosopher Seneca's wise observations on the virtue of gratitude and the vice of ingratitude. "He that bestows a favor must not at once act the part of a punisher of ingratitude, but rather that of a kindly physician, by healing the ingratitude with repeated favors."[17] Perhaps if we, even while lonely, can continue to reach out and do good deeds, even for those who give us little thanks or pay us little heed, we will act as kindly physicians toward ourselves as much as toward our ungrateful neighbors.

[17] *ST*, II-II, Q. 107, art. 4.

Prudence

Prudence is the fourth and final cardinal virtue. Also known as *practical wisdom*, it is referred to in the *Catechism of the Catholic Church* (CCC) as "the charioteer of the virtues" (no. 1806) because of the way it guides the implementation of the other cardinal virtues of temperance, fortitude, and justice, as well as their bevy of allied virtues. Prudence is both an intellectual and a moral virtue because it determines moral means to moral ends and guides us in acting on them. Thomas, following Aristotle, also calls prudence "right reason applied to action." Prudence is a virtue that gets the job done, finding the right and virtuous means to achieve virtuous ends. Of course, any Catholic experiencing loneliness will seek prudent means of ending it or making it more bearable.

Thomas describes prudence's "parts," which are allied virtues, or capacities required to make the virtue of prudence fully operational. Let's peek at them one by one and see how they might be employed by the lonely (or by those seeking to alleviate another's loneliness):

1. *Memory* is the first part of the virtue of prudence because, to achieve virtuous goals in the future, we must act in the present, guided by the lessons we have learned in the past. Some modern research shows that the chronically lonely can develop selective memories, emphasizing negative past experiences when they were ignored, rejected, or perhaps even bullied, making them more hesitant to risk reaching out to others. If we are to cultivate the virtue of prudence in ourselves in a way to help remedy loneliness, we must be diligent in reminding ourselves or reminding lonely loved ones of the many positive interpersonal

experiences most likely experienced but perhaps for-gotten. Can you recall any right now?

2. *Understanding* refers to the capacity to apply universal principles we have grasped to particular situations. In combating the distress of loneliness, this could entail training ourselves to see how our possible tendencies to awfulize automatically or perhaps to personalize appar-ent slights from others may be operating in particular interactions, leading us to neglect the possibility that others' behavior might have been prompted by some-thing impacting them and not because of us.

3. *Docility* is the willingness to be taught by others. In quaint and touching language Thomas explains that "in matters of prudence man stands in very great need of being taught by others, especially by old folks who have acquired a sane understanding of the ends in practical matters."[18] What especially strikes me here is the language about "old folks." One hallmark of our culture seems to be the glorification of youth and the neglect or denial of aging. To what lengths do we go to avoid looking our age? Yet, it is encouraging that in the research involving people's confidants, one class of confidants that remained relatively stable from 1985 to 2004 was that of one's parents.[19] If you are experienc-ing loneliness and are still blessed to have a parent or another older confidant, have you sought that person's wisdom? Chances are they have experienced some

---

[18] *ST*, II-II, Q. 49, art. 3.
[19] See "Recent Loneliness Studies Make the Headlines," at the end of chapter 5.

loneliness too. The practice, per Thomas, is also quite biblically sound! " 'Thus it is written: Lean not on thy own prudence' (Prov. 3:5) and 'Stand in the multitude of the ancients (i.e., the old men), that are wise, and join thyself from thy heart to their wisdom' (Sirach 6:35)." Indeed, by tapping into the rich resources of the wisdom of the elderly you may well be applying some balm to their own loneliness.

4. *Shrewdness* refers to the ability to reason one's way quickly to appropriate actions when there is no opportunity, time, or need to seek someone else's guidance. Perhaps in regards to loneliness, shrewdness can be built by training yourself so your automatic thoughts in social situations are not ones that lead to distress or inaction.

5. *Reason* refers to the ability to get at truths by step-by-step rational processes, starting with the information we glean from our senses, as opposed to the kind of direct intuition and knowledge enjoyed by the angels, who are purely spiritual beings. Of course, the proper use of reason to guide our emotions and behaviors is a cornerstone of the kinds of cognitive therapies we examined in our last chapter and even the name of Ellis's Rational Emotive Behavioral Therapy starts with an adjectival form of the word *reason*. If we are to be prudent in interpersonal situations, we will train ourselves not to jump to conclusions, as if we had the awesome intuitive powers of the angels or the limited instinctual responses of the animals, but to reason things out one step at a time! We will heed God's advice to use carefully the great gift of reason that He gave us alone among all the

creatures on earth: "Come now, let us reason together, says the LORD" (Isa. 1:18).

6. *Foresight* is truly integral to and almost synonymous with prudence. Since prudence seeks present means to future ends or goals, we need the capacity to predict the future impact of the means we choose to employ. Thomas first cites St. Isidore, who wrote that "*a prudent man is one who sees from afar (porro videns): and this is also the derivation from providentia (foresight) according to Boethius.*"[20] One way we can train ourselves in foresight is to imagine the possible consequences of any actions we might take to alleviate our loneliness, in terms of other people's reactions, while we train ourselves at the same time to cope rationally and calmly with whatever kind of response actually comes to pass. Further, it implies that when we try to "see afar" into the future, we do so with clear glasses, so to speak, and not with dark lenses, expecting to see the worst.

7. *Circumspection* cannot be circumvented if we seek to act prudently to relieve our own or a neighbor's loneliness. Just as foresight tries to find means that are *by their nature* suitable for their ends (for example, displaying love and care toward a neighbor), circumspection, which means seeing "all around" an issue, also considers whether otherwise appropriate means should not be employed in favor of others that fit the particular circumstances. Thomas provides an interesting example: "Thus to show some signs of love to someone seems, considered in itself, to be a fitting way to arouse love

---

[20] *ST*, II-II, Q. 49, art. 6.

in his heart, yet if pride or suspicion of flattery arise in his heart, it will no longer be a means suitable to the end."[21] There may well be times when initiating and reciprocating friendly overtures to some people will not be prudent ways to cope with loneliness, especially if we have reason to believe the intentions of our behaviors will be misinterpreted.

8. *Caution* must not be thrown to the wind if we are to act prudently in social situations. Thomas explains that matters requiring prudent action can be quite contingent and complicated. Sometimes "evil has the appearance of good. Wherefore, prudence needs caution, so that we may have such a grasp of the good as to avoid evil."[22] When we exercise the caution of prudence, we will look before we leap into behaviors, relationships, and commitments that might on the surface look like good remedies for loneliness, but which we sense might contain perils that warrant a pause for a deeper look.

How to Connect with Others through God and the Theological Virtues

Faith is the first of three special virtues infused into our souls by God at our Baptism. We'll dig into the rich theology of the virtue of faith in a bit, but I'd like to begin by noting that the relevance of one's religious faith to the experience of loneliness has not been ignored by modern psychotherapists. In one insightful analysis from the 1980s, two social psychologists examined a

---

[21] *ST*, II-II, Q. 49, art. 7.
[22] *ST*, II-II, Q. 49, art. 8.

variety of interrelationships between religious faith and loneliness and their implications for psychotherapy.[23]

The authors provide brief accounts of actual case studies that illustrate how different kinds of religious beliefs and behaviors interact with different kinds of loneliness.

- In the worst case, they mention a person who joined a religious cult out of a simple desire to acquire new friends to overcome his loneliness.

- Another young man underwent an intense religious experience and a feeling of "oneness with God" that prompted him to turn intentionally away from others and isolate himself as he attempted to recreate that experience.

- In a perhaps more common scenario, a young man who felt lonely and unloved became a member of a church and began to participate and contribute his skills and efforts to the church's group activities.

- A married couple who grew up in a small town and had actively participated in the activities of the same local church all their lives reported that they have never felt severely lonely.

- A woman who believes that she has a personal relationship with God and speaks to Him often through prayer reported that this helps her feel less lonely.

- A young man joined and devoted great efforts to a social cause, spurred by his religious beliefs, and acquired such

---

[23] Raymond F. Paloutzian and Aris S. Janigan, "Interrelationships between Religiousness and Loneliness," in *Psychotherapy and the Lonely Patient*, edited by Samuel M. Natale, 3–14 (New York: Harrington Park Press, 1986).

a deep sense of purpose that he thinks less about his problems and feels less lonely than he did before.

These examples illustrate different ways in which people's religious beliefs and behaviors can impact the extent to which they feel lonely and what they do about it. Coming from the perspectives of social psychology, the authors view "religiousness" through psychological glasses. They see it as a personality attribute or trait that can impact all kinds of beliefs, thoughts, feelings, and behaviors. Further, they cite psychologist Gordon Allport's distinction between "extrinsic" and "intrinsic" religious motivations, which can be measured on a continuum. Those with a more extrinsic religious orientation tend to use their faith itself as a means to an end, practicing religion for some kind of practical personal or social benefit, whereas those with an intrinsic religious orientation have internalized their beliefs at the core of their being and strive to live their faith. Allport argued that intrinsic, lived religion serves as a "master motive" that guides other attitudes, feelings, and actions. Recognizing that "intrinsic religion" can supply relief from loneliness, the authors suggest that therapists might help lonely religious clients who are found to have a more extrinsic religious orientation (using assessment scales developed by psychologists) by trying to redirect them toward the deeper commitment of an intrinsic orientation.

This is all interesting and relevant in terms of *psychological* perspectives on religion and loneliness, but the *theological* lenses of St. Thomas Aquinas can shed far greater light on the loneliness-healing power of "intrinsic religion." Thomas wrote extensively about religion as a virtue. When we develop the virtue of *religion*, we strengthen our disposition toward honoring God through external acts such as communal worship and sacrifices and internal acts such as personal prayer and devotions. These are means to the ends of an even higher virtue, the virtue of *faith* itself.

Faith is the first of three theological virtues described for us by St. Paul: "So faith, hope, and love abide, these three; but the greatest of these is love" (1 Cor. 13:13). Faith, hope, and charity embody "intrinsic religion" at the depths of our innermost being. They join our souls to God. Indeed, per the *Catechism:* "They are the pledge of the presence and action of the Holy Spirit in the faculties of the human being." They are the "master motive" at its most masterful: "They inform and give life to all the moral virtues. They are infused by God into the souls of the faithful to make them capable of acting as his children and of meriting eternal life" (no. 1813).

Faith

Faith, the first of these virtues, lays the foundation for all the virtuous actions of a Christian. Reason provides the foundation for natural moral virtues. Faith does not contradict reason but lifts it to higher realms of truth revealed by God, truths that human reason cannot scale without God's aid. The God-given virtue of faith then comes to inform and direct the natural cardinal virtues and all their fellow flyers by helping us grow in our knowledge and love of God, the Source of all that is right and good. St. Thomas declares, echoing St. Augustine, that "there are no real virtues unless faith is presupposed."[24] After all, we cannot hope for heaven or love God with all our hearts and our neighbors as ourselves if we don't know and believe in Him first!

---

[24] *ST*, II-II. Q. 4, art. 7.

The virtue of faith is also foundational to a Catholic approach to loneliness. It holds open the door to the highest and most important of all human experiences, our connectedness with our heavenly Father and with our neighbors on earth as our brothers and sisters in Christ. In this way, it is our faith in God and in the teachings of His Church that can provide us with the wisdom and strength we need to defeat or endure loneliness.

Hope

Hope appears in the secular psychological literature on loneliness. A recent study of Israeli middle school students showed two key factors in lessening the likelihood of loneliness: a personal tendency toward hopefulness and a "cohesive" family environment with close bonding between family members.[25]

High levels of hope have been found to be associated with positive outcomes in all kinds of areas, including academic and athletic performance, physical and mental health, responsiveness to psychotherapy, and in helping inoculate children from feelings of loneliness.

So the human psychological disposition toward hope, a belief that one has what it takes to devise and carry out the plans to achieve one's goals, appears to confer substantial benefits, including protection from loneliness.

Still, the *theological virtue of hope* bespeaks a far higher power than that of our own capacities! With the God-given theological virtue of hope our hopes for positive outcomes in the future extend to the most positive of all outcomes, bliss with God in

[25] Cited in Ami Rokach, ed., *Loneliness Updated: Recent Research on Loneliness and How It Affects Our Lives* (New York: Routledge, 2013), 62.

heaven for eternity! Further, through the theological virtue of hope we need not depend merely on our own feeble powers, but can rely on the omnipotent power of God Himself, so that we can say with St. Paul: "I can do all things in him who strengthens me (Phil. 4:13). *The theological virtue of hope presupposes our desire to spend eternity with God and our confidence that He will help us get there through the grace of the Holy Spirit.* If we have truly embraced the virtue of hope, we will be far less daunted by the transient sufferings we may endure in our time on earth, including the trials of loneliness.

Still, even on a natural plane, our God-given capacity for the human *passion* of hope, our inborn inclination to strive for good things even when they are difficult to obtain, can help connect us to others. Thomas writes: "Love is caused by hope, and not vice-versa, because by the very fact that we hope that a good will accrue to us through someone, we are moved towards him to our own good; and thus we begin to love him."[26] When we look with hope upon another person as a possible source of something good *for us*, our natural inclination to love ourselves and want good things for ourselves will inspire us move *toward that other person with love* as a source of good to us. Such hope can lead to the kind of openness, trust, and generosity through which the mutual love of friendship can grow.

Charity

Charity, the highest of all virtues, holds the ultimate key to unlocking satisfying and meaningful interpersonal relationships and dispelling the distress of loneliness. As St. Paul tells us, "If I

[26] *ST*, I-II, Q. 40, art. 7.

... have not love ... I am nothing.... If I ... have not love, I gain nothing" (1 Cor. 13:2–3). Charity is expressed in the greatest of the commandments in the words of Christ Himself: "You shall love the Lord your God with all your heart, and with all your soul, and with all your mind. This is the greatest and first commandment. And a second is like it. You shall love your neighbor as yourself" (Matt. 22:37–39; cf. Luke 10:27; Mark 12:30–31). If the world lived out these two commandments of charity, how could we possibly speak of a worldwide epidemic of increasing loneliness?

Many are the ways in which the hot fires of charity and the warm joys they bring can melt away the sad, cold isolation of loneliness. "Charity," again per St. Thomas, "is the friendship of man for God."[27] In chapter 4 we will examine how human friendships grounded in such charity can help us banish loneliness. Charity is at the heart of the greatest and newest commandment: "A new commandment I give to you, that you love one another; even as I have loved you, that you also love one another" (John 13:34). The life and actions of Christ Himself have become our standard and models for how we are to express that love for one another on earth. It is to those loving lessons of Christ and how they can dispel loneliness that we'll turn in chapter 5.

In our next chapter, we will take an important respite from our search for interconnection to consider the potential solaces of solitude. Are there psychological and spiritual benefits that might be gained from time spent alone, either freely chosen or imposed from outside by events that might give rise to loneliness? Let's look inside ourselves and see.

---

[27] *ST*, II-II, Q. 23, art. 1.

Action Plan

Read. The most succinct Catholic introduction to the moral and theological virtues is found within 11 pages or so in the *Catechism of the Catholic Church*, part 3, article 7, "The Virtues," numbers 1803–1845. Perhaps the most thorough Catholic treatment of these virtues is found in approximately 700 pages of the second part of the second part of St. Thomas Aquinas's *Summa Theologica*, available in many editions, including free online versions. There are many wonderful and accessible modern Catholic treatments of the virtues, including philosopher Josef Pieper's *The Four Cardinal Virtues* and his *Faith, Hope, and Love*; Fr. Romano Guardini's *Learning the Virtues That Lead You to God*; and Professor Mitchell Kalpakgian's *The Virtues We Need Again* and *The Virtues That Build Us Up*.

Reflect. Think about the connections between what modern psychologists call adaptive social cognition and the nature of moral virtues as described by St. Thomas Aquinas. We will live happy, holy lives when our passions are appropriately moderated and controlled by our God-given reasoning abilities. Further, think about the eight parts or related virtues that are required for the full exercise of prudence, or practical wisdom. Do you need to fix or reorder any of those parts so that you can make better practical choices in alleviating your loneliness?

Remember. Well, here we go again. You will recall that St. Thomas said that memory is the first and most essential part of prudence. Virtues are strengthened through practice, and, because they perfect our human powers, they bring a special sense of satisfaction and fulfillment when they are exercised. Can you train yourself to recall times when you have felt joy from acting virtuously or from being treated virtuously by others? Of course you can. Then go out and produce some new joy born of virtue by doing some act of kindness or generosity the next opportunity you have to interact with another person.

Recite. We saw that we Christians have an advantage regarding virtues such as wisdom in our ability simply to ask our generous God for them in steadfast faith, and He will give them to us (cf. James 1:2–5). There are classic Catholic prayers that request God's assistance in growing in virtue. St. Thomas Aquinas's prayer "Pro Obtinendus Virtutibus" (To Acquire the Virtues) includes such eloquent and moving requests as these:

> *Grant that I may abide*
> *on the firm ground of faith,*
> *be sheltered by an impregnable shield of hope,*
> *and be adorned in the bridal garment of charity."*[28]

There are also traditional Catholic prayers for the theological virtues of faith, hope, and charity; for example, the Act of Charity:

> *O my God, I love Thee above all things,*
> *with my whole heart and soul,*
> *because Thou art all good and worthy of all love.*
> *I love my neighbor as myself for the love of Thee.*
> *I forgive all who have injured me,*
> *and ask pardon of all whom I have injured.*

---

[28] *The Aquinas Prayer Book*, 33.

Reconnect. A most special way in which Catholics can reconnect with God and neighbor is through the sacraments Christ gave us to be shared through the communal acts of His Church. Further, theologians have long noted the relationship between the sacraments and the virtues, highlighting the connections between Baptism and faith, Confirmation and fortitude, Reconciliation and justice, Matrimony and temperance, Holy Orders and wisdom, Anointing of the Sick and hope, and the Eucharist and charity.

So then, we can help break free from loneliness by remembering our bonds with our brothers and sisters in Christ through sacraments such as our Baptism and Confirmation and by availing ourselves of God and our fellow members of the Body of Christ by attending Mass, receiving Christ in the Eucharist, and confessing our sins, growing in virtue thereby. One very simple step, if daily Mass is not possible for you, is to consider arranging your schedule to attend at least one weekday Mass in addition to Sunday Mass.

Loneliness and Mental Disorders

Psychoanalyst Frieda Fromm-Reichmann argued decades ago that loneliness can sometimes play an important role in the genesis of serious psychiatric disorders. Loneliness is not considered a diagnosable mental disorder, but it may lead to or flow from some mental disorders, and even if it does not, it may produce great suffering itself. So, even though most of us who are lonely at times will not cross the threshold into a mental disorder, it is worthwhile to know where loneliness stands in relation to some psychiatric maladies, lest we or a loved one cross that border at some time and might benefit from professional mental health treatment.

People with mental disorders are often very lonely. Loneliness itself does not appear as a symptom that leads to the diagnosis of major mental disorders, but it often accompanies them.

Loneliness may be a risk factor for and found along with a variety of mental disorders, the most common of which is depression. The hallmark of depression is sadness, and people who feel very lonely rarely feel very happy about it. There can be overlap between feelings of loneliness and depression and also some confusion in distinguishing the two.

Perhaps the fundamental distinction between the two is that the sadness of loneliness is more precisely limited to those perceived deficiencies in emotional and social relationships, whereas the sadness of depression is far more global, affecting virtually every area of one's life.

The lonely person may feel sad that he has no one to confide in or may feel out of place in a group, but the depressed person will feel sad about life in general. The lonely person may feel of little worth in certain social situations, perhaps when he is not chosen for a team or spoken to at a party, whereas the depressed person may ruminate about his worthlessness all the time.

If you feel you may be seriously depressed, a consultation with your general physician or a mental health professional (preferably a psychiatrist or a clinical psychologist) is highly recommended. Depression can have very serious consequences and can often be successfully treated.[29]

Another condition that shares much in common with loneliness is that of grief or bereavement. A reaction of grief or bereavement at the loss of a close loved one, especially a spouse, is a universal and normal reaction to one of life's most powerful traumas, since loved

---

[29] I also direct readers to Aaron Kheriaty, M.D., and Fr. John Cihak, S.T.D., *The Catholic Guide to Depression: How the Saints, the Sacraments, and Psychiatry Can Help You Break Its Grip and Find Happiness Again* (Manchester, NH: Sophia Institute Press, 2012) for a thorough and masterful examination of the psychological and spiritual dimensions of depression by a psychiatrist and a priest.

ones are among God's greatest gifts to us as wayfarers on earth.

Loneliness is also a part of the grieving experience, but what distinguishes grief or bereavement from loneliness itself is that while the other common stages or reactions typically diminish with time as one adjusts to the loss, loneliness may well continue if a new intimate relationship is not formed. In this way, bereavement can be a risk factor for that most intimate variety of loneliness, emotional isolation.

Another mental disorder that can share some features with loneliness is social anxiety disorder, or social phobia. Distinguishing criteria of this disorder include a marked fear or anxiety about being observed and scrutinized by others in a variety of social situations requiring interaction (as in conversation), being observed (as when eating or drinking), or in performing in front of others (as in giving a speech).

This condition might call to mind the old-fashioned, commonsense term *shyness*. The tendency to be more shy or withdrawn in certain social situations is a normal personality trait that need not be negative. Sometimes, of course, quieter folks sit back, observe, and absorb while other, more extroverted types are more comfortable taking center stage.[30] Social anxiety disorder is more extreme and distressing than normal shyness.

---

[30] That this kind of behavior may have its advantages can be seen from the wisdom of old adages ("Still waters

Even people who are not normally particularly shy or socially fearful can come to display some of those characteristics in more severe cases of loneliness. People experiencing intense or prolonged loneliness often come to feel more vulnerable in social situations, and their emotions and thought processes can become distorted in the face of the feelings of insecurity that come from a perceived lack of connections with others. If their early attempts to remedy their loneliness are not successful, lonely people may respond by becoming too critical or suspicious of others. Over time they may become increasingly more defensive, hypersensitive to criticism, negative, avoidant, withdrawn, isolated, and less capable of forming new relationships.

Unfortunately, such behaviors tend to drive others further away from them, creating a vicious circle and self-fulfilling prophecy of sorts. This by no means implies that loneliness cannot be conquered, though, even among those most anxious around others.

I will also note again that if a reader is feeling seriously distressed by a depressive or anxiety disorder, by a prolonged bereavement, or by intense, prolonged loneliness,

---

run deep") to Scripture ("Be quick to hear, slow to speak" [James 1:19]) to Abraham Lincoln's quip "It is better to remain silent and be thought a fool, than to speak out and remove all doubt!" See Proverbs 17:28: "Even a fool who keeps silent is considered wise; when he closes his lips he is deemed intelligent."

or if such a condition is seriously impairing his ability to function in the normal activities and duties of life, consultations with a physician or mental health professional is recommended.

Chapter 3

The Solace of Solitude

Whilst it is certainly more difficult for most people
to find meaning in life if they do not have close
attachments, many people can and do lead equable
and satisfying lives by basing them upon a mix-
ture of work and more superficial relationships.

— Anthony Storr, *Solitude*

The angel afterwards told him [St. Kevin] to go into the
desert glen which had been foretold to him, that is to the
slope of the lakes. Great was his courage afterwards in
separating from the glory and beauty of the present life,
and remaining in solitude listening to the converse of the
angel who ministered to him.... He spent seven years in
this manner of solitude far from the society of men.

—Charles Plummer, *Lives of the Irish Saints*

Alone but Not Lonely

As it is possible to feel isolated and lonely in the midst of a crowd, so too, *it is possible to spend great swaths of time by oneself without feeling lonely.* This has not escaped the attention of modern psychiatrists and psychologists or of ancient sages and saints from millennia ago from all around the globe. In this chapter, we will examine some of the many potential advantages of solitude, of time spent alone, whether or not initially of one's own choosing, for healing and transforming the distress of loneliness. We will examine solitude in light of the theories of psychiatry, the lives of worldly men and women of creative genius, the lives of great Christian hermits and saints from the sandy deserts of the Middle East to the forests of Russia, to a strikingly beautiful "glen of two lakes" on the east side of the Emerald Isle. Finally, we will consider solitude's potential blessings and solace within the privacy of your own room.

The Lone Genius

In the British psychiatrist Anthony Storr's influential book *Solitude*, first published in 1988, he sought to provide some balance to what he felt was an inordinate emphasis upon the importance of interpersonal relationships to human psychological health. He certainly did not discount the immense role that close connections with others play in human well-being, but he feared that for some people, anyway, close relationships do not necessarily play such an essential role, and it could be harmful to overemphasize such a need, implying that something is wrong with them.

Storr cites a seemingly overlooked paper, a "psychoanalytic classic," Donald Winnicott's "The Capacity to Be Alone,"[31] published at virtually the same time that Frieda Fromm-Reichmann was drawing attention to loneliness in psychoanalytic circles. Winnicott argued that while a substantial body of psychoanalytic literature had focused on the *fear* of being alone or the *wish* to be alone and to be separated from others, as seen in some psychiatric disorders, it was time that the *positive aspects* of the *ability* to be alone were examined.

Psychoanalysis, first developed and heavily influenced by Sigmund Freud, had greatly emphasized the importance of interpersonal relationships to emotional health, although Freud himself, when once asked the most important constituents of psychological health, replied the ability to *love* and to *work*.

Although Storr does not cite him in this context, as a graduate of the Adler School of Professional Psychology in Chicago, I feel obliged to note that Alfred Adler, one of Freud's earliest colleagues, would later develop his own unique system of psychotherapy with even more emphasis on the value of healthy interpersonal relationships.

For Adler the most fundamental hallmark of psychological health was what the Austrians term *gemeinschaftsgefuhl*, typically translated as "social interest" and sometimes as "communal

---

[31] Donald Winnicott, "The Capacity to Be Alone," *International Journal of Psychoanalysis* 39 (1958): 416–420.

feeling." A person is psychologically healthy when his or her goals, strivings, and actions in life have the well-being of others in mind.[32] Still, given this essential role for relationships, Adler (in a sense, one-upping Freud) spoke of what he called *three* fundamental and unavoidable "life tasks": *love, work,* and *communal life.* Perhaps the tasks of love and communal life will call to mind the experiences of the loneliness of emotional and social isolation that can arise when they are thwarted. Note, too, that Adler, like Freud, also considered *work*—some kind of a productive occupation—essential to mental health. Adler roots even work in the social context, though, noting that we are dependent on others for basic needs such as food, shelter, and clothing, and we are obliged to play our part in serving the needs of others.

Storr emphasizes the relatively overlooked importance of productive work to mental well-being. He notes that for some psychologically healthy people, engrossing work may play a more prominent role in their lives than maintaining particularly close interpersonal relationships. People more inward or introverted by temperament may seek out long periods of solitude so they can immerse themselves in their work. Such solitude often serves others out in society quite well in the long run.

Among Storr's examples is that of Sir Edward Gibbon (1737–1794), who remained a bachelor, and though he enjoyed socializing at times, chose to live predominantly an isolated life of study that led to lasting historical and literary contributions that

---

[32] Adler's standard of mental health essentially echoes the message of Christ's second great commandment: "You shall love your neighbor as yourself" (Matt. 22:39; Mark 12:31, Luke 10:27; cf. Lev. 19:18).

people still read to this day.[33] Other examples of men whose lives of comparative solitude led to notable works and achievements include Sir Isaac Newton and the philosophers Immanuel Kant, Henry David Thoreau, and Ludwig Wittgenstein.

Further, even unchosen, enforced periods of solitude have yielded great contributions to mankind. The Roman philosopher Boethius (ca. 480–524), whose book *On the Trinity* was later cited by St. Thomas Aquinas, wrote his famous *Consolation of Philosophy* while he was isolated in prison pending his execution. St. Thomas More (1478–1535), author of *The Sadness of Christ*, which we'll look at in this book's chapter 5, also wrote *A Dialogue of Comfort against Tribulation* while, like Boethius, he was imprisoned pending his execution. Sir Walter Raleigh (1554–1618) wrote *The History of the World* during an imprisonment, like More's, in the Tower of London, his confinement lasting thirteen years. During four years in a Siberian prison, Fyodor Dostoyevsky (1821–1881) thought out three stories and two novels and made notes for his *House of the Dead*, which would describe his prison experience. Closer to our time, Alexander Solzhenitsyn's (1918–2008) imprisonment and exile by the Soviets would give rise to *Cancer Ward* and *The Gulag Archipelago*.

Still, of course, one would hope to avoid forever an enforced solitude of the kind experienced by the prominent men described above. Neither need one be a creative genius to profit from solitude. Further, there are many kinds of "work" that might make up the life task of a Christian, depending on his or her calling from God. Next, we'll look at the solace of solitude in the lives of a

---

[33] Indeed, quite coincidentally, as I look to the right on my desk right now, I spy volume 1 of his epic *Decline and Fall of the Roman Empire*, which I've been rereading with profit and enjoyment!

small sample of saints who listened for the "still small voice" of God (see 1 Kings 19:12) while alone in some manner of wilderness.

The Solitude of Sanctity: In the Desert, Forest, and Glen

Inspired by Christ who, after His Baptism, was led by the Holy Spirit into the wilderness, where he fasted and was tempted by the devil (Matt. 4:1; Mark 1:12; Luke 4:1–2), many men and women in the first centuries sought seclusion in the deserts of the Middle East, in modern-day Egypt, Syria, Turkey, and other lands, where they too might fast and pray as Christ did. Some had experienced great difficulties living the life of Christ in the world and were instructed by the words of St. James: "Unfaithful creatures! Do you not know that friendship with the world is enmity with God? Therefore whoever wishes to be a friend of the world makes himself an enemy of God" (James 4:4). They interpreted this in their own cases as a call to remove themselves from the hustle, bustle, and noise of the world so that they might heed God's voice in solitude.

Some of the most influential of these people came to be known as the Desert Fathers. Some lived the eremitic life,[34] becoming full-fledged hermits, living alone at least at times, while others adopted a cenobitic life,[35] living in monastic communities in which the monks would spend most of their time in their own small huts and meet on occasion for communal activities. These hermits and

[34] From the late Latin *eremitia* and earlier Greek *eremites*, *eremitic* (of the desert), applied to desert-dwelling hermits.
[35] From the late Latin *cenobita* and earlier Greek *koinobion*, from *koinos* (common) and *bios* (life), *cenobitic* applied to those who lived in a communal arrangement.

monks knew well that to remove themselves from the world was certainly not to remove themselves from all temptation toward sin. Indeed, Matthew, Mark, and Luke all describe how, during Jesus' forty days of prayer and fasting in the desert, He was tempted by the devil. Some of these Desert Fathers, such as Evagrius of Pontus (345–399), and St. John Climacus (525–606), would provide the Church with some of her most profound insights into the nature of temptation and sin and how best to combat them.[36]

Modern author (and sometimes hermit) Peter France, in his 1996 book *Hermits: The Insights of Solitude*, makes a very important point about how, throughout history, those who have chosen to live outside the world often end up with a great deal to offer those still immersed in the world:

> Those who have chosen to live outside society have always been eagerly sought out for advice on how to live within it. Hermits have built up great reputations not only, as might be expected, for heroic asceticism or spirituality but for insight into the ways of the world. They have often found it difficult to preserve their seclusion from the crowds who came to disturb it in search of counsel. They have something to say to us today even in an age so uniquely adverse to solitude.[37]

The ancient Desert Fathers' contemplations have provided a rich treasury that the Church has pulled from again and again across the centuries. In the thirteenth century, for example, two

[36] See the former's *Practical Treatise* and the latter's *Ladder of Divine Ascent.*
[37] Peter France, *Hermits: The Insights of Solitude* (New York: St. Martin's Press, 1996), xiii.

religious orders emerged on the scene at the same time to bring the gospel *out into the world*. The Franciscans and the Dominicans, unlike traditional religious monks and church canons, who were stable in their attachment to a monastery or a cathedral, would bring the gospel to the people of the countryside and the cities and minister to them in the needs of their daily lives, from the education of their children to hospital care for their sick and dying. Even these dynamic orders, so immersed in the world,[38] would draw on the rich lessons of those ancient solitary hermits and monks of the Eastern deserts.

Blessed Humbert of Romans (1193–1277), for example, was the fifth master general of the Dominicans (officially, the Order of Preachers), an order that strives to share with others the fruits of contemplation. In his masterful *Treatise on the Formation of Preachers*, he draws from the contemplation of the Desert Fathers when he explains that sometimes preaching will not be successful when people come to hear it only out of curiosity or to be entertained. He relates a story from *The Lives of the Desert Fathers* in which some brothers and secular religious went out to hear the fourth-century Desert Father Abba Felix. Abba Felix sat silent for a long time and then told them that when people come to hear but are not prepared to practice what they hear, God removes the grace of preaching from the elders and they have nothing to say!

France highlights another similar tradition in the *startsy* (singular: *starets)* of the Russian Orthodox Church, perhaps best known through the character of Zosima in Fyodor Dostoyevsky's novel *The Brothers Karamazov*. The word means "elder," deriving

---

[38] With the exception of some cloistered, contemplative groups even within these orders.

from the Russian word for "old," and the *startsy* are monks or hermits, often living deep in the forests, whom other religious and people of the world seek out for spiritual and practical guidance, including areas such as work and relationships. There was a major revival of the *startsy* tradition in Russia during the nineteenth century, around the time when Dostoyevsky wrote. Perhaps the most powerful and influential spiritual treatise associated with the *startsy* is the anonymous nineteenth-century Russian book *The Way of the Pilgrim*.[39]

We've dipped into the deserts and forests, and now it is time to take a peek at another interesting hermit, who lived in the "glen of two lakes." Christ commissioned His disciples to preach the gospel to all nations unto the ends of the earth. In the fifth century, the isolated island of Ireland was, for all practical purposes, one of those ends of the earth. A land of pagan Celtic religion, it extended beyond the borders of the great Roman Empire and would never become a part of it.

Most interestingly, the island's conversion was largely the result of one of those unchosen, enforced solitudes like the involuntary imprisonments we have examined. In this one, a boy of almost sixteen within the borders of the Roman Empire is kidnapped by Irish raiders, along with thousands of his countrymen, to be enslaved across the sea in Ireland. There, during nearly seven years of captivity, and often of solitude, the boy would come to

---

[39] This captivating book starts with a man's desire to understand St. Paul's exhortation in 1 Thessalonians 5:17 to "pray constantly." The man becomes a spiritual pilgrim, who travels to various churches and monasteries, seeking to find the answer. He eventually meets a *starets*, who teaches him the simple "Jesus Prayer," a variant of "Jesus Christ, Son of God, have mercy on me, a sinner," building on the tax collector's words in Luke 18:13.

pray to God while alone in the mountains, herding sheep, "a hundred times a day and as many times at night."[40] When he finally escaped and returned home to the island of Roman Britain, it was not long before he burned with desire to return to the land of his captivity and bring to those people the gospel of Christ. This boy, of course, is now known as St. Patrick, and soon, through his powerful evangelization, his adopted land of Ireland would become known as an island of saints and scholars.

There is a very rich tradition of a vast number of Irish saints who lived in the early generations after St. Patrick, and many were drawn to the monastic life, not yet in vast monasteries, but in communities of huts situated around a church. One of the most serious seekers of solitude among them was my namesake, St. Kevin of Glendalough (ca. 498–618).

Glendalough is pronounced "glen' duh lock" and means the glen, or narrow valley, of two lakes (*da lough*). Situated southwest of Dublin in the county of Wicklow in the east of Ireland, it is described in some modern travelers' guides as one of the most beautiful sites in all of Ireland, and I certainly agree.

St. Kevin is among a vast number of saints whose stories are captured in the fascinating and sometimes whimsical "ancient lives" of Irish saints, some in Gaelic and some in Latin, that were written or translated in the late Middle Ages, many centuries after these saints' deaths. St. Kevin's story is full of intriguing events, among which were prophecies attributed to St. Patrick and even to the pagan giant hero Finn MacCumhail, that a great man such as Kevin would come to live in that valley and turn it into a great city.

[40] We are blessed to have this boy's story in his own words in his *Confessio*.

To make a long story of countless tales short, Kevin was trained as a monk, and when his studies were completed, he headed out to the wild "desert glen" of this chapter's opening quotation. He slept in a sliver of a cave on a cliff over the upper of two lakes, using a rock for his pillow. Each morning he'd cross the lake without a boat and say Mass all by himself. A frequent pastime was to pray while standing immersed in the waters of the lake. Notice, too, from our quotation, that, like Jesus, to whom "the angels ministered" in the desert (Mark 1:13), St. Kevin enjoyed angelic company.

Kevin's passionate desire for solitude is highlighted by many stories, including that of one amorous young lady named Kathleen "with eyes of unholy blue," per one account, who was drawn to the saint by his beauty and grace. As the legend goes, he eventually had to drive her away with a switch of sharp nettles! Good at heart, she later came to appreciate the saint's spiritual beauty surpassing his physical charms and became a religious herself.

Perhaps the most important story, though, for our purposes is that of how St. Kevin's nearly complete solitude was ended. Another of his favorite devotions was to sit in study and prayer within the confines of the hollowed trunks of great trees. The legend goes that one day a prosperous "one-hundred *kine* [cow] farmer" brought his cows to graze in Kevin's glen. One cow would wander deep into the woods, go up to the saint praying in the tree, and begin to lick his feet. When the cow came back each night, it would produce the milk of fifty cows! The farmer had to get to the bottom of this and sent a trusted servant to follow the cow. When the servant discovered Kevin, the saint so desperately sought not to be revealed that he promised the man a place in heaven if only he'd keep quiet! This was to no avail, though. They found the great saint so emaciated from his prayer and fasting that they had to carry him out on a litter.

Kevin was then willing to end his perpetual solitude, for it was prophesied that he would build a great city (monastery) in that glen. This he did, and over the centuries it grew to house seven churches, a great 110-foot stone tower that still stands, and a cemetery within which Irish kings would be buried. For centuries, it was the home of great yearly festivals, and even today it's a popular site for tourists and pilgrims.

Kevin's story illustrates the power of chosen solitude for some as a means for deeper communion with God. Even after he had come out of the woods, however, St. Kevin would still go back for periods of prayer and fasting, especially during Lent. In perhaps the most famous episode, as he stood praying in a little hut with his arms extended out the windows in the cross-vigil position, like Christ on the Cross, a blackbird laid her eggs in his hand. Kevin, a great lover of all God's creatures, did not move his arm until the eggs hatched and the birds flew away. Here is how one ancient life tells it in meter in the words of the saint, who was always thinking of Christ and open to redemptive suffering:

> Alas! a pain greater than the requital
> My hand like a log under the blackbird:
> The blood of His hands, of His side, of His feet
> The King of Heaven shed for my sake.

Kevin's penitential solitude prepared him for the works of God and the service of his neighbor. God had plans for him, and as the legend related through the words of his angel:

> The angel said expressly:
> "Though shalt not be torturing thyself any longer:

Depart from thy bondage without delay,
Thy business is ready with God."[41]

Perhaps from St. Kevin we all can learn the power of periods of chosen solitude to commune with God and with His creatures in nature to renew and recharge ourselves for the tasks God has planned for every one of us, whether or not we might be alone or feeling lonely, for He and His angels are always with us.

Just You and God Together in Your Own Room

Perhaps the most extreme, or at least unusual, example of chosen solitude was that of St. Simon Stylites (390–459), who felt besieged by the pressures of the world and took up residence on a small platform with a railing that he constructed atop a pillar amid ruins in Syria, near Aleppo, a city unfortunately besieged by the ravages of war in our time. For more than thirty years, he lived atop a series of pillars from nine to fifty feet tall! Nonetheless, for St. Simon, Peter France's words ring loud and clear, for even when Simon was atop his pillar, people flocked to him for advice and, thankfully, to hoist food and other necessities to him.

Does perching upon a pillar just for an hour or two sound appealing to you, at least once in a while? It does to me, and I have to wonder whether some of those monastic round towers in Ireland functioned not only as bell towers, watchtowers, fortresses, and storage bins but also as lofty heights on which some secluded reflection and prayer was obtained.

---

[41] Both quotations are in Charles Plummer, *Lives of the Irish Saints*, vol. 2 (1922; repr., New York: Oxford University Press, 1997), 137.

Of course, we do not need a sandy desert, a dense forest, a wild glen, or a tall tower, let alone a fifty-foot pillar, to avail ourselves of the psychological and spiritual solace of solitude. Recall that when Jesus Himself advised us about prayer, He said simply: "When you pray, go into your room and shut the door and pray" (Matt. 6:6).

Many great saints seeking solitude have heeded precisely this simple advice. St. Catherine of Siena (1340–1387), for example, did not escape the notice of Anthony Storr, who wrote the book on *Solitude*: "St. Catherine of Siena spent three years in seclusion in her little room in the Via Benincasa during which she underwent a series of mystical experiences before entering an active life of teaching and preaching."[42] St. Rose of Lima (1586–1617) patterned her life on St. Catherine's and spent vast amounts of time praying in her room or in a tiny shed, barely largely than a closet, in her backyard. She too was blessed with mystical ecstasies. One of our most recent Doctors of the Church, St. John Avila (1499–1569), as a young man returned to his father's home and "the next three years were spent almost entirely in the seclusion he made for himself, with the consent of his parents, in his father's house, and in which he devoted himself to the practice of penance and to the study of the science of the saints with our Lord and His Blessed Mother as his chief teachers."[43]

We may not experience miraculous ecstasies while immersed in solitude, but if we seek out a place in our homes where we can turn off all electronic distractions and be by ourselves to pray, to do spiritual reading, or just to sit and think, we will be in the

---

[42] Anthony Storr, *Solitude: A Return to the Self* (New York: Free Press, 1998), 34.

[43] *Finding Confidence in Times of Trial: Letters of St. John of Avila* (Manchester, NH: Sophia Institute Press, 2012), ix.

best possible situation, perhaps outside of our church, to hear God speak to us in a still, small voice. We will know we are not alone, and the counsel we may receive might well help us cope with our own loneliness or awaken in us ways to reach out to a lonely person in our lives.

Action Plan

Read. Spiritual reading of all kinds is an excellent way to enhance the solace of solitude and to build your capacity to be alone. First and foremost is the thoughtful reading of Scripture each day, whether you select passages spontaneously, adhere to a guided plan,[44] or follow the daily Mass readings. Also, consider reading about some of the great saints known for their pursuit of holiness through solitude, at least during parts of their lives, such as the Desert Fathers and Sts. Catherine of Siena, Kevin of Glendalough, Rose of Lima, and John of Avila, who were mentioned in this chapter.

Reflect. Rethink the way you look at your time as an opportunity for spiritual growth, a time for reconnection with God that will charge your spiritual batteries for when you go forth into the world to reach out and reconnect with others.

Remember. Think back on times when you achieved solace, comfort, and strength from periods of solitude. Where were you? What were the circumstances? What did you do in those times

---

[44] See, for example, Vicki Burbach, *How to Read Your Way to Heaven* (Manchester, NH: Sophia Institute Press, 2017).

you spent alone? Then set aside some time to create new soul-building periods of solitude and spiritual retreat.

Recite. Of course, solitude can provide the perfect opportunity for prayerful communion with God. Cultivate the practice of spontaneous conversation with God, and also consider the use of formal prayer books that link us in prayer to the universal Church and the great communion of saints who have joined in the same prayers over the centuries and across the globe. In this sense, even in prayers prayed in periods of solitude, we are never truly alone.

Reconnect. When your spiritual batteries have been recharged, do what you can with your own personality and life circumstances to be like a St. Kevin emerging from his tree or a St. Catherine from her room, sharing God's love and mercy with every person you encounter.

Is Loneliness in Our Genes?

To get a fuller grasp of the nature of loneliness, we should take a quick look at the effects of genetics and environment—nature and nurture, if you will—in determining the likelihood that a person will experience serious loneliness. Of course, after looking at the possible genetic influence of a condition such as loneliness, we will remember that even for people with a strong tendency toward loneliness there are certainly effective ways to prevent or allay it.

Although specific identified genes may produce some medical disorders, such as the neurological illness of Huntington's disease, we can point to few, if any, specific genes that necessitate a complex psychological state such as loneliness. Many illnesses, especially psychiatric disorders, seem best explained by what is called the diathesis-stress model. The *diathesis* (from the Greek for "state" or "condition") is a predisposition, such as a person's genetics, that sets a sort of threshold. Crossing that threshold because of serious or persistent stressors may result in a mental disorder.

For example, perhaps a person has a family history of schizophrenia. He might have a low threshold due to those genetics, and if he encounters serious problems in life, he might develop schizophrenia. If he does not encounter such stresses, however, or even learns ways effectively to cope with stress, schizophrenia may never develop. Indeed, even within sets of identical twins, who share all the same genes, if one twin is diagnosed with schizophrenia, there is only a 50 percent chance that the other twin will also be schizophrenic.

Genes seem to play a powerful role here, but *far from an all-powerful* role. The "heritability" (the proportion of variance in a population that can be attributed to genes) of schizophrenia has been estimated at around 0.8, meaning that it contributes about 80 percent, leaving the other 20 percent of variance to other causes. Nurture—that is, one's environment, one's life situation, social supports, coping strategies, and so forth—can still play a role that makes all the difference.

Although much research remains to be done, it appears that the tendency toward loneliness also runs in families. Based on various studies, researchers have estimated its "heritability" at around half of that found for schizophrenia. One study I came across estimated that both parental loneliness and shared family environment together accounted for only 18 percent variance in determining whether a person would experience significant loneliness as a young adult.[45]

In other words, some people may have a moderately strong genetic tendency to feel lonely. Researchers aren't sure why, but some speculate that it could be because of differences in genes that influence and regulate certain

[45] Rokach, *Loneliness Updated*, 129.

combinations of brain neurotransmitters or other chemicals such as oxytocin that seem to play a role in experiencing human attachment.

The future will certainly tell us more about the story of the genetics of loneliness, but we already know that genetics will never be the *full* story when it comes to experiencing or alleviating loneliness. Whether or not you might have a stronger genetic tendency to experience loneliness, there is plenty you can do about it, with the grace of God, to help keep you under the threshold of distressing loneliness.

Chapter 4

He Came to Call Us Friends

A faithful friend is a sturdy shelter;
he that has found one has found a treasure.

—Sirach 6:14

It is written (John 15:15) I will not now call you servants
... but my friends. Now this was said to them by reason of
nothing else than charity. Therefore, charity is friendship.

—St. Thomas Aquinas, *Summa Theologica*, II-II, Q. 23, art. 1

Here we are, you and I, and I hope a third,
Christ, is in our midst.

—St. Aelred of Rievaulx, *Spiritual Friendship*

Jesus Our Confidant

Modern research has confirmed that a growing number of people feel that they have few, *if any*, people to confide in. The ability to confide in another; to bare our hearts, express our worries, concerns, and passions; and to seek and to give acknowledgment, support, and advice are among the hallmarks of friendship. Depending on their nature and intensity, friendships can provide remedies, or at least soothing balms, to the loneliness of both emotional and social isolation.

Of course, the greatest gifts can produce the greatest sorrows if they are lost or if they seem forever out of reach. Perhaps you have lost a great friend and confidant, perhaps even a husband or wife with whom you have shared all the good things (and hard times) of life for many years. Perhaps, for whatever reason, you feel that you don't have a friend in the world. There is still no need to despair of the joys of true spiritual friendship with another person at some time in the future, and always with Jesus Christ, right now.

Christians know, but perhaps do not always consider, that Christ is always there for us to confide in, to be our dearest friend who cares for our well-being with unbounded love. As Jesus Christ told us and as Sts. John and Thomas Aquinas remind us, the son of God came to earth and took on human form so that we would be not servants but friends. Indeed, He performed that greatest act of friendship for us all, to "lay down his life for his friends" (John 15:13). Christ is there for us as our greatest friend.

In this chapter, we will focus on the lessons we can learn from the way Christ Himself endured the cross of loneliness. We will look at one of the most joyful blessings God has shared with us to keep loneliness at bay. Hopefully it will inspire us to cherish and honor any deep friendships we have lost and will buoy our spirits. Hopefully too it will inspire those who question whether they have any friends at all to reach out in small ways to establish the beginnings of what could become a great remedy for loneliness: your own, and perhaps that of your new spiritual friend.

Insights into Friendship

Although there will be no loneliness in heaven in the company of God and the great communion of saints, God provides us with real remedies for the pains of loneliness while we live out our lives here on earth. St. Thomas notes that "if we speak of the happiness of this life, the happy man needs friends."[46] Thankfully, God has given us the capacity to form bonds of friendship with one another that can heal and lighten lonely hearts. Scripture abounds in praise of earthly friendships and provides some wonderful examples, most notably, perhaps, the friendship between David and Jonathan in the Old Testament and of Christ and His disciples in the New. They provide examples of tremendous mutual care, support, and even tenderness, as when the beloved disciple John, at the Last Supper, reclined *in sinu Jesu*, "close to the breast of Jesus" (John 13:23). The wisdom literature of the

[46] *ST*, I-II, Q. 4, art. 8.

Old Testament, especially Proverbs and Sirach, also abounds in rich sayings that sing the value of human friendships.

The examination of human friendship itself has a very long and profound history. Indeed, I don't think it is very widely known, but the two most profound and influential classical pagan philosophical writings on friendship from the years before Christ were later completely absorbed, commented upon, Christianized, and perfected independently by two Catholic saints, one a Cistercian and the other a Dominican.

Let's examine these writings now, with a special focus on how these four perspectives on friendship might help us all defeat loneliness.

Virtuous Friendship

Friendship was a common and important theme among classical philosophers. Even ancient Stoic authors, who stressed the self-sufficiency of the "wise man," who truly *needs* nothing other than the pursuit of virtue to live a good life, argued that such a man would certainly also *desire* and *choose* to have friends if he could. Indeed, this was sometimes expressed in the noblest of ways. Seneca, for example, explicitly contradicts a saying of Epicurus to the effect that we seek friends to stay by us when we are ill and to help us when we are in need. Seneca proclaims, rather, that *we seek friends in order to have someone to sit by when he is sick and to help when he is in need.*[47] (What a remedy to loneliness would friends like that provide!)

---

[47] Seneca, *Epistles 1–65*, trans. Richard M. Gummere (Cambridge, MA: Harvard University Press), 47.

The Greek philosopher Aristotle (384–322 B.C.) wrote the most thorough and foundational ancient treatment of friendship in books 8 and 9 of his *Nicomachean Ethics*, immediately after his chapters on virtues. Previewing themes he will later develop, Aristotle talks of friendships within families, among citizens, among fellow travelers, and even in a limited sense among animals. Indeed, he was no stranger to the value of emotional and social connections at all levels.

After explaining that through love we are attracted to things, either because those things are *pleasant* to us, *useful* in some way, or because they are *good* in themselves (or at least *seem* good to us), Aristotle launches into perhaps his most famous and thought-provoking contribution to the understanding of friendship, namely, the classification of three kinds of friendship: friendship of utility (*sumpheron*), friendship of pleasure (*hedon*), and friendship of virtue (*arête*).

We all have human friendships based to some extent on utility. We tend to befriend (and be befriended by) those who can be helpful to us, or whom we can aid in some way. Friendships built in school or in the workplace often start at this level. We gravitate toward those who might be able to give us a little help or advice, or perhaps toward those to whom we can offer some expertise. This is all fine and good, as far as it goes, but utility is the lowest rung of the ladder of friendship. When taken to an extreme, it may not represent much of a friendship at all. Consider the "user," who values a friend only for what the "friend" can do for him. What happens if you are no longer of use to the user? No, true friendship, as an embodiment of charitable love, is not entirely about one's own benefit.

A next step up the ladder is friendship based on pleasure. It says not only, "I value what you can do for me," but, "Your presence is pleasant to me." This may build upon the first level of friendship. Perhaps your friend first helped you learn to play a certain sport, and now you enjoy pursuing it together with him, and even just talking about it. This tells your friend that you value not only what he has done or can do for you but also something about his person.

At this level of friendship, you acknowledge that there are things in the other's personality or character—perhaps a sense of humor, hopefully an embodiment of some talent or virtue—that make it pleasant for you to be around him. But this level of friendship also has its limits. It still says that you value your friend for what he gives you: in this case, not help but pleasure. What will happen to your friendship if he ceases to please you (or you cease to please him)?

The third and highest level of friendship is the friendship of virtue. This is the friendship that truly embodies human excellence. The true friend has a love and concern for the welfare of his friend. The focus of this friendship is not on the good you can receive but on the good you can give to another. Aristotle notes that "very likely friendships of this kind are rare." His main reason for saying this? "Virtuous men are scarce." You see, to have a loving friendship based on one's own virtue and the love of the virtue in another, the friends themselves must be virtuous.

Is not Aristotle's classification of friendship a call to classify our own friendships and our own roles in them? Which of our friendships are friendships of excellence or virtue, those being the only complete, perfect, or true friendships? Have we sought out virtuous friends? Have we worked to acquire the virtues that can make us good friends to others?[48]

---

[48] In previous chapters of his *Nicomachean Ethics*, Aristotle described eleven moral virtues (courage, moderation, liberality,

Aristotle compares and contrasts the types of friendships and declares that not only are virtuous friendships *the best,* but because of the stability of character that virtue brings, they are also *the most enduring,* as long as the friends continue to express their affection through ongoing interactions.

As to how such friends treat one another, Aristotle says that a friend becomes like "a second self," so truly virtuous friends treat one another as they would treat themselves.

He proceeds to list defining features of friendship with others but first notes that these characteristics all derive from how we relate to ourselves: we wish to continue to exist, wish for good things, take actions to achieve them, take pleasure in our own company, and seek to be of one mind about important things. He then lists five elements of friendship deriving from self-love:

- A friend desires his friend to be, to exist.
- A friend desires good things for his friend.
- A friend does good deeds for his friend.
- A friend takes pleasure in his friend's company.
- A friend is of one mind with his friend, rejoicing and sorrowing in almost the same things.

These are five things that virtuous friends wish for and do for their friends.

The first can be clearly seen in cases of the loss of a good friend, in the anguish and loneliness we experience when a good friend no longer exists. We wish our friends to exist for their

---

magnificence, greatness of soul, ambition, gentleness, friendliness, truthfulness, wittiness, and justice), as well as intellectual virtues (science, understanding, wisdom, art, and prudence, the practical wisdom that lies at the crossroads of both intellectual and moral virtue). You will notice the overlap with many of the virtues we discussed in chapter 2.

own sakes, and when they die, it can feel as if we've lost part of our self. Of course, our desires do not determine reality, and sometimes our friends will die before we do. In these cases, we would do well to imagine ourselves from our deceased friend's perspective. Would he or she want us to be mired in grief, or to reach out to others and enjoy life again?

Although incomplete in itself (because it can arise for people we do not even know and lacks in itself the familiarity necessary to the intense love and desire of friendship), *eunoia* (goodwill) for others, as we have for ourselves, is an element of true friendship and is especially necessary for the development of new friendships.

When we have goodwill for our friends, we wish for them the same kinds of good things we wish for ourselves. Of course, if we truly wish good things for our friends, we will take actions to try to achieve them. Aristotle examines the exchange of benefits between virtuous friends, too, noting that *beneficence*, the giving of benefits or doing of good deeds for our friends, is truly something fine and noble. Further, the giver of benefits therefore feels pleased with the person he has been able to benefit. The friend has afforded him the opportunity to exercise his beneficence. In that sense, the benefactor has also benefited himself. Such repeated acts of friendship lead to *homonoia*, a sameness, harmony, or concordance of desires and aspirations, so that friends grieve and rejoice at the same things, bespeaking of their emotional closeness.

These are just a few of the highlights of Aristotle's exhaustive analysis of friendships that we might mine for remedies for loneliness. One point worth emphasis is how the most complete and satisfying of friendships are those built on virtue. Do you recall the psychologist's sample self-statement in our chapter 1 for combating the feelings of loneliness that can lead to over-eating? One thing the lonely person was advised to repeat to himself was that "rather than feeling sorry for myself, I will work on making myself the most attractive and interesting person I can be." For Aristotle, the undisputed key for making oneself most truly "attractive and interesting" to others is to become more virtuous.

Another point to consider is that Aristotle addresses the question as to whether he should even grant the name of friend-ship to friendships based on pleasure or use, and he concludes that these imperfect forms of friendship still do deserve the name. Sometimes the simple shared pleasures, aid, or support provided by less-than-perfect friends can provide solace and help bridge the gap of emotional and social isolation. Further, sometimes friendships built at first upon some shared enjoyment or mutual benefit can blossom into more fulfilling friendships of virtue if the friends are open to growing together in virtue as well as in friendship. If you are lonely, are you open to establishing new friendships of use or pleasure with the hope that through your efforts and God's grace they might flower into new friendships of virtue?

Harmonious Friendship

The other great ancient treatise on friendship was penned by Roman orator and philosopher Marcus Tullius Cicero (106–43 B.C.). Variously entitled in translations On Friendship, Laelius on Friendship, and sometimes simply the Laelius, the book is a literary dialogue on its face, but the character of Laelius holds the floor for the vast majority of the text while his sons-in-law Quin-tus Mucius Scaevola and Gaius Fannius Strabo mainly provide background information, ask him questions, and prod him to continue to share of his thoughts on friendship.

The book's namesake, Gauis Laelius Sapiens the Younger (ca. 190–after 129 B.C.) earned the cognomen or nickname "Sapiens," "the Wise," both for his political and military prowess and for his broad philosophical learning. Laelius was known as the close friend of the Roman general and twice consul Scipio Africanus Minor, son of Scipio Africanus, the revered military strategist who defeated Hannibal of Carthage in North Africa (hence his cognomen "Africanus"). Cicero's dialogue takes place shortly after and is occasioned by the younger Scipio's somewhat suspicious sudden death in bed in 129 B.C., which prompts Laelius to speak at length on the nature and nurture of friendship to honor his closest friend after his death.

There is little doubt of the value Laelius (and Cicero) placed on friendship by the brief definition and assessment provided: "For friendship is nothing else than an accord in all things, human and divine, conjoined with mutual goodwill and affection, and I am inclined to think that, with the exception of wisdom, no better thing has been given to man by the immortal gods."[49] Although Cicero does not directly reference or quote Aristotle, his views on friendship are largely consistent with Aristotle. It is because of his great emphasis upon harmony or concordance in will and affection between friends that I refer to it as "harmonious" friendship to contrast with Aristotle's "virtuous friendship," bearing in mind that neither neglects the importance of both harmony and virtue to true friendship. Cicero's paean to friendship is elegant, enlightening, and encouraging. Laelius's grief and loneliness at

[49] Cicero, *On Friendship*, trans. W. A. Falconer (Cambridge, MA: Harvard University Press, 2001), 131.

the loss of his dear friend Scipio is made bearable and sweetened by the memories of Scipio he can cherish in his heart and share with others, like his young sons-in-law.

A modern translator opines on the excellence of this work: "Certainly no other author of ancient or modern times has discussed the subject of friendship with so much completeness and charm as Cicero discusses it in his *Laelius*."[50]

I will not elaborate more on Cicero's writings on friendship here because a great, though relatively little-known Catholic saint was as charmed by them as the modern translator and would build a Christianized version of friendship upon its edifice in the most remarkable way more than a millennia after Cicero and almost nine hundred years ago today.

Spiritual Friendship

St. Aelred of Rievaulx (1110–1167) spent his youth at the court of King David of Scotland, eventually as his chief steward. In his early twenties, in 1132, Aelred was sent out on some business involving Archbishop Thurstan of York and visited the Cistercian abbey at Rievaulx. He was so taken by his day with the monks that after sleeping on it but one night he presented himself at Rievaulx for admittance as a monk. In the ensuing years, the young monk was sent to Rome to help with negotiations regarding Archbishop Thurstan's successor and had a fateful meeting with St. Bernard of Clairvaux on his way back. By age thirty-three he was sent to lead a group of monks in founding a new abbey at Revesby, and at age thirty-seven, in 1147, he was called back to Rievaulx as their abbot, a position he held until

[50] Ibid., 106.

his death twenty years later. Abbot Aelred ruled the monastery, wrote a number of spiritual and historical books, and clearly developed and cherished his own friendships all the while.

Aelred had been deeply moved by Cicero's writings on friendship and wrote: "I acquired Cicero's famous book on friendship, and at once it seemed to me both useful in its weighty thoughts and pleasant in its agreeable eloquence."[51] Years later, though, after his deep conversion to Christ he wrote: "These ideas I had gathered from Cicero's treatise on friendship no longer had for me their wonted savor. For now nothing which had not been sweetened by the honey of the sweet name of Jesus, nothing which had not been seasoned with the salt of Sacred Scripture, drew my affection so entirely to itself."[52]

Aelred then proceeded to write his own dialogue on friendship, *De Spirituali Amicitia* (*Spiritual Friendship*), openly building upon Cicero, incorporating nearly one-third of the Roman's text, but transforming it in the most delightful ways, bringing new and supernatural light to the ancient classical wisdom. Although there is clearly an elegance of style in Cicero's *De Amicitia*, there is not much true dialogue, Laelius dominating the conversation in what is almost a monologue. When we read Aelred's *Spiritual Friendship*, though, it is as if we are eavesdropping on real intimate conversation between friends earnestly discerning just what friendship is. It is friendship in action, experienced and brought to life in text. I can't help but agree with this assessment from a modern commentator: "It is Aelred, not Cicero, who makes

[51] St. Aelred of Rievaulx, *Spiritual Friendship*, trans. Mark F. Williams (Chicago: University of Scranton Press, 2002), 27.

[52] Aelred of Rievaulx, *Spiritual Friendship*, trans. Mary Eugenia Laker S.S.N.D. (Kalamazoo, MI: Cistercian Publications, 1977), 46.

friendship seem something so timeless and universal that one is tempted to ignore its historical context."[53]

So, what are a few of Aelred's key insights on spiritual friendship, and how they might help conquer loneliness? The most important and unique feature of Aelred's *Spiritual Friendship* jumps to the fore in the very first sentence after his prologue, when he declares that there are he and his friend Ivo, and he hopes that a third, namely, Christ, is right there with them. Aelred did not cite the verse, but clearly knew well Christ's words that "where two or three are gathered together, there am I in the midst of them" (Matt. 18:20). Clearly, then, this presence of Christ is something Aristotle and Cicero never wrote about or thought about, having died before Christ's birth. Although Aelred notes openly that he owes much to Cicero for his understanding of friendship, his friendship with Jesus Christ has totally transformed the meaning of friendship and made it immeasurably more "*dulcis*" — sweeter, dearer, and more delightful to him. Clearly, Aelred is going to present his case that Christ did not come to abolish friendship, so to speak, but to completely fulfill it![54] It is God become man, Jesus Christ, who forges the bonds of true friendship between

---

[53] Brian Patrick McGuire, *Friendship and Community: The Monastic Experience, 350–1250* (Ithaca, NY: Cornell University Press, 2010), 326.

[54] Some people in the monastic tradition were suspicious of the idea of "particular friendships" between the religious, influenced by texts such as James 4:4: "Do you not know that friendship with the world is enmity with God? Therefore, whoever wishes to be a friend of the world makes himself an enemy of God." Some theologians in the East and the West interpreted these words as a condemnation not only of inappropriate *worldliness*, but of individual *friendships* in the world. They believed that when a man left the world to embrace the life of spiritual per-

people in friendships that center on Him and His love. Aelred also makes clear how Christocentric true friendship is, declaring that friendship must begin with Christ, continue with Christ, and be perfected by Christ.

Aelred, like Aristotle, goes on to describe three classes of friendship: false *carnal* or fleshly friendships based on mutual seeking of illicit pleasures; *worldly* friendships based upon mutual worldly gains; and true *spiritual* friendship.

Spiritual friendship, the only one Aelred calls true, desires no worldly gains and seeks no extrinsic purpose, but arises from its own intrinsic dignity, and the warmth of the human heart, so that its fruit and reward are nothing other than friendship itself. Building upon Cicero, he then provides his own definition: "And so spiritual friendship among the just is born of a similarity in life, morals, and pursuits; that is, it is a mutual conformity in matters human and divine united with benevolence and charity."[55]

Spiritual friendships are also friendships of virtue, but of supernatural as well as natural virtue, the highest of them all being charity. Aelred provides a Christian understanding of virtue not to be seen in Aristotle or Cicero. As for *acquiring virtue*, we saw that Aristotle wrote that to build enduring dispositions toward virtue we must repeatedly perform acts of virtue, as builders become builders by building and harpists by playing the harp. Aelred, however, notes that Christians need not despair of acquiring the virtues necessary for true friendship, because virtue is there for the asking: "Ask, and you shall receive" (Matt. 7:7; John 16:24). It is Christ Himself, the source and bond of Christian friendship, who

---

fection, friendships and family ties should be severed and not replaced.

[55] Laker's *Spiritual Friendship*, 61.

spoke these words to us. We see the same advice applied to that highest virtue of wisdom in James: "If any of you lacks wisdom, let him ask God, who gives to all men generously and without reproaching, and it will be given him" (James 1:5).

Aelred would certainly not deny, however, that we must play our part in cooperating with such gracious gifts, as his treatise on friendship itself is also very focused on the kinds of actions friends must perform to build and sustain spiritual friendships. He makes the bold declaration that although Cicero might declare only three or four notable friendships were proclaimed throughout history in his time, Christians can cite *thousands* of pairs of friends made possible through Christ's grace. We might ask ourselves if we are open to forming new bonds with our brothers and sisters in Christ that might place us within those numbers.

With God's great gift of spiritual friendship available to us to enjoy and to share, and with insights like Aelred's a part of the Church's repository of holy wisdom for nearly nine hundred years now, how sad to think that so many Christians, indeed so many Catholics, are lonely today. St. Aelred believed that God has formed us to seek out such bonds. We need to ask ourselves if we are heeding Christ's call to love our neighbors as ourselves if we don't strive to break people's chains of loneliness to replace them with bonds of spiritual friendship.

Charitable Friendship

Close friends often share the same interests in the most important of things: "kindred spirits" they may be called. How interesting that in the history of the philosophy and theology of friendships, there are two relatively independent pairings of "kindred spirits," each separated in their lives on earth by more than one thousand years. (We can hope they have now made each other's acquaintance in heaven!) We have seen how St. Aelred was so moved by the writings of Cicero and, through the grace of Christ, would elevate friendship to a far higher and holier level.

Now we will consider how St. Thomas Aquinas did virtually the same thing to the writings on friendship of Aristotle.[56]

St. Thomas would draw extensively from Aristotle, for example, from his description of three kinds of friendship, and from the five ways in which the love of others in friendship grows from our natural inclination to love ourselves. As for St. Thomas the man himself, his own natural temperament and inclinations led him to embrace solitude, preferring to spend vast amounts of time in prayer and in study. There are also many incidents describing him as an absentminded professor of sorts, so deeply absorbed in thought at times that he forgot he was with other people. Still, Thomas had some notable friendships, including, during his youth, with his great mentor, St. Albert the Great, and later in life with his *socius* (close companion) within the Dominican Order, Reginald of Piperno. Also, Thomas wrote that better even than contemplation was to share with others the fruits of one's contemplation, and he literally practiced what he literally preached, through many years of preaching and university teaching.

Among the lessons Thomas taught that might help us assuage loneliness in ourselves and in others are those in the *Summa Theologica* on charity, the highest of all virtues. Indeed, Thomas

[56] Unfortunately, it does not appear that St. Thomas, whose knowledge was most encyclopedic, was aware of St. Aelred and his major works, *The Mirror of Charity* and *Spiritual Friendship*. It appears that copies of Aelred's works were rare in the first centuries after his death, with circulation limited to a few Cistercian monasteries.

chose to start his lengthy examination of charity by showing how charity is really a state of friendship between man and God, citing 1 Corinthians 1:9: "God is faithful; by Whom you are called unto the fellowship of His Son. Love based on this friendship is charity; wherefore it is evident that charity is the friendship of man for God."[57]

How close in thought this is to that of St. Aelred, who notes the affinity between charity and friendship. As Jesus' beloved disciple John said of charity "God is love," Aelred's friend Ivo asks him whether it might be said that "God is friendship." Aelred replies that such an inference is certainly unusual and not found clearly in the Scriptures, "but still what is true of charity, I surely do not hesitate to grant to friendship, since 'he that abides in friendship abides in God, and God in him.'"[58]

Thomas, too, notes the deep intertwining of charity and friendship; charity, as he stated, essentially being friendship with God. This friendship with God has extremely intense and far-reaching implications for friendships here on earth and the dispelling of loneliness. In some of his most poignant lines, St. Thomas famously compares charitable love to the heat of a powerful furnace.[59] When our hearts burn with the fires of charity, their far-reaching flames serve to warm strangers and even our enemies. But since those closest to the furnace receive the most heat, true charity should begin at home, and be directed in greatest intensity to those who are near to us: our spouses, families, friends, school- or workmates, neighbors, and fellow parishioners. We would do well to heed this last point in striving

---

[57] *ST*, II-II, Q. 23, art. 1.
[58] See 1 John 14:16.
[59] *ST*, II-II, Q. 27, art. 7.

to help the lonely, since it is not only the bereaved or the isolated who may feel lonely, but even our family members.

We need to ask ourselves if we have truly been sharing the heat of loving charity with those closest to us. Have we paid enough loving attention to discern a face of loneliness living in our own house, perhaps our spouse or our child? If so, we must take action, as St. Thomas advises: "The love of neighbor requires that not only should we be our neighbor's well-wishers, but also his well-doers."[60]

So, what exactly are the kinds of actions we can take to alleviate the loneliness of our neighbor, whether that neighbor is a half a world away or sitting across the room? We'll consider at least thirty ways in chapter 6. But just before that, we'll look at the life of Jesus Christ on the earth and on the Cross and see what He can teach us about bearing loneliness when it may be the cross we are called to carry.

Action Plan

Read. Read St. Aelred of Rievaulx's beautiful *Spiritual Friendship* and his masterful *Mirror of Charity*. The latter book, written at the insistence of and starting with a letter by St. Bernard of Clairvaux, explains how Christ's yoke is light because it is the yoke of charity. Read also St. Thomas Aquinas's treatise on charity in his *Summa Theologica*, II-II, questions 23–46, for a magnificent and nuanced approached to exactly what we owe God, neighbor, and self through the charity that is friendship with God.

---

[60] *ST*, II-II, Q. 32, art. 5; cf. 1 John 3:18.

Reflect. Think about your current friendships. How would you classify them according to Aristotle's categories of friendships of *use*, *pleasure*, or *virtue* or according to St. Aelred's categories of *carnal*, *worldly*, or *spiritual* friendships? If some friendships are less than perfect, ask yourself what you might do to move them toward a more virtuous, spiritual plane? If you feel you are bereft of friends at this time, ask yourself with whom you might strive to build a new virtuous, spiritual friendship, even if it is to be built upon the foundation of some shared wholesome pleasure or mutual benefit at first. Consider too that all spiritual friendships are ultimately founded upon and united with Jesus Christ.

Remember. Think back to your most satisfying friendships with your peers, family members, or perhaps a teacher, a priest, or some kind of mentor. Thank God for those friends, and even if you no longer have them, thank God for the time when you did. Let these recollections motivate you to reach out to forge new friendships and strengthen old ones.

Recite. Pray to God that your friendships will be strengthened and that you will form new ones. Pray for your friends as well. St. Anselm of Canterbury (1033–1109) wrote a powerful, poignant prayer for our friends. Here is a most moving excerpt:

> My good Lord, as your servant I long to pray to you for my friends, but as your debtor I am held back by my sins. For if I am not able to pray for my own pardon, how then can I dare to ask openly for your grace for others? If I anxiously seek intercessors on my own behalf, how then shall I be so bold as to intercede for others? What shall I do, Lord God, what shall I do? You command me to pray for them and

my love prompts me to do so, but my conscience cries out against me, saying that I should be concerned about my own sins, so that I tremble to speak for others. Shall I then leave off from doing what you command because I have done what you have forbidden? No, rather since I have presumed so greatly in what is forbidden, all the more will I embrace what is commanded. So perhaps obedience may heal presumption, and charity may cover the multitude of my sins.

So I pray you, good and gracious God, for those who love me for your sake and whom I love in you.

Reconnect. Now go and reach out to old friends and new. Cherish a friend, as wise Seneca advised, not as someone to tend to you when you are sick, sad, or lonely, but as someone whom you can tend to in his or her times of need and loneliness.

Have We Crafted a "Culture of Loneliness"?

"We risk becoming a nation in which everyone feels a little neglected, a little left out. And we will all feel that it has been done to us, not by us."[61]

Of this you can be certain: *if you are lonely, you are not alone*. Loneliness has always been with us, but it is very important to consider that the prevalence of loneliness seems to be escalating at an alarming rate in our time. A recent review of dozens of studies on loneliness done throughout the world in recent decades forewarns: "Researchers have predicted that loneliness will reach epidemic proportions by 2030 unless action is taken."[62] It appears we are on a trajectory for a veritable epidemic of loneliness in a decade or so unless something can be done to stem the tide. What is it about our modern world that, as population soars, increasingly higher percentages of people report that they feel emotionally and socially isolated from others?

---

[61] Jacqueline Olds and Richard Schwartz, *The Lonely American: Drifting Apart in the Twenty-First Century* (Boston: Beacon Press, 2009), 21.

[62] Juliann Holt-Lundstad, Timothy B. Smith, Mark Baker, Tyler Harris, and David Stephenson, "Loneliness and Social Isolation as Risk Factors for Mortality: A Meta-Analytic Review," *Perspectives on Psychological Sciences* 10, no. 2 (2015): 236.

A number of secular books from the 1960s onward have argued that American culture has been moving away from meaningful traditional social bonds and interactions toward self-absorption and consumerism. For example, in 1979, historian Christopher Lasch wrote the bestseller *The Culture of Narcissism: American Life in an Age of Diminishing Expectations*. He argued that absorption in the self and in the consumption of material products had followed in the wake of the crumbling of the family and traditional communal values. Less than two decades later, in March 1995, Pope (and now St.) John Paul II made widely known another crucial "culture of" phenomenon engulfing and corroding interpersonal relationships in the modern world, a "culture of death":

> This culture is actively fostered by powerful cultural, economic and political currents which encourage an idea of society excessively concerned with efficiency. Looking at the situation from this point of view, it is possible to speak in a certain sense of a war of the powerful against the weak: a life which would require greater acceptance, love and care is considered useless, or held to be an intolerable burden, and is therefore rejected in one way or another. A person who, because of illness, handicap or, more simply, just by existing, compromises the well-being or life-style of those who are more favoured tends to be looked upon as an enemy to be resisted or eliminated. In this way a

kind of "conspiracy against life" is unleashed. This conspiracy involves not only individuals in their personal, family or group relationships, but goes far beyond, to the point of damaging and distorting, at the international level, relations between peoples and States.[63]

Might not this worldwide "culture of death" that values production and efficiency over the love and care of all human life contribute to growing loneliness, especially among those frail, weak, elderly, or disabled persons seen by many as burdens on society? Of course, Pope John Paul II was a dynamic champion of a "culture of life" to counter it, a culture that valued every human life in and of itself from conception until natural death. Quite fascinatingly, when in a 1991 interview secular author Christopher Lasch was asked where he saw signs of "hope" or "moral vision," he responded that while there was "not much" present in organized religion, "one finds flashes of it in the Catholic tradition. . . . One might even say that the Pope has some of the best insights into social questions"—a rather surprising answer for a former Marxist imbued with radically secularist ideals from childhood.[64]

---

[63] John Paul II, *Evangelium Vitae*, March 25, 1995, no. 12, http://w2.vatican.va/.

[64] The summary and comments are from Jeremy Leer's "The Radical Lasch," *American Conservative*, March 27, 2007, http://www.theamericanconservative.com/.

Truly, John Paul II was as much a sage as a saint.

We may ponder to what extent our modern culture of consumerism, of narcissism, of technological efficiency, and, most sadly, of death has contributed to loneliness in our time. That we are immersed in a "culture of loneliness" seems hard to argue in the light of mountains of social science data.

In the year 2000, political scientist Robert Putnam's *Bowling Alone: The Collapse and Revival of American Community* documented significant declines in America during the last century in participation in a vast array of human social connectedness, including associations with political parties, civic groups, church affiliation, workplace associations, informal social associations, and more.[65] His memorable title reflected his finding that while, for example, the sport of bowling was thriving at the time of publication, fewer people than ever before bowled in organized leagues, preferring to "bowl alone" or with a select group of friends. Further, he noted that even some people still in formal leagues might as well have been "bowling alone," as they watched big-screen TVs between their turns instead of socializing.

Of course, his findings went far beyond bowling leagues to all kinds of formal and informal associations and activities, including organized political activities,

---

[65] Robert D. Putnam, *Bowling Alone: The Collapse and Revival of American Community* (New York: Simon and Schuster, 2000).

card playing, going on picnics and other group out-
ings, simple visits to friends, dinners out with friends,
and even family dinners at home. People had become
increasingly likely to spend their spare time at home and
oftentimes alone.

Chapter 5

The Loneliness of Christ

Jesus said to him, "Friend, why are you here?" Then they came up and laid hands on Jesus and seized him.

—Matthew 26:50

"I do not know the man."

—Matthew 26:74

Theologians and spiritual writers alike are prepared to say that the loneliness of Christ during his Passion and death outweighed his physical agonies.

—Hubert Van Zeller, O.S.B., *The Mystery of Suffering*

Loneliness and Redemptive Suffering

Although God has made us to share eternal happiness with Him in heaven, the path to heaven for us wayfarers here on earth is often strewn with serious troubles that can lead to true suffering. As Christians who trust in God's plan for us, we can rest assured, as St. James told us, that such trials and tribulations can serve a real purpose for our greater good in the end, helping to perfect us. Still, if it was easy to "count it all joy" (James 1:2) when faced with the trials and tribulations that arise from loneliness, there would be little need for books like this one!

Nonetheless, our Catholic approach to loneliness can provide us succor from its sufferings that secular approaches cannot. In the wise words of philosopher Peter Kreeft:

> You see, the Christian views suffering, as he views every-thing, in a totally different way, a totally different context, than the unbeliever. He sees it and everything else as a *between*, as existing between God and himself, as a gift from God, an invitation from God, a challenge from God, some-thing between God and himself. Everything is relativized. I do not relate to an object and keep God in the background somewhere; God is the object that I relate to. Everything is between us and God.... My very I is his image, not my

own but on loan. What then is suffering to the Christian? It is Christ's invitation to us to follow him. Christ goes to the cross, and we are invited to follow to the same cross. Not because it is the cross, but because it is his.[66]

This ability to see suffering on earth as part of our relationship with God and something willingly taken on and endured by Christ Himself for our sake can revolutionize our understanding of our own suffering and of the suffering of others. It gives us a greater power to endure our suffering and to see the inviolable worth of every other human person's life, also enmeshed in intimate relationship with God. It has far-reaching implications for our lives and the lives of our neighbors. It helps us to see that the person who suffers near the end of life is still always worthy of life until its natural end, that the person in the womb who might be likely to suffer from some genetic malady or from poverty is still always worthy of a chance to experience his or her own gift of life from God. It can help us bear our own loneliness and strive to lighten the burden of the loneliness of our neighbor.

The source of this ability to bear our own cross is the gift of grace of God through the action of the Holy Spirit stirring in our souls. The ultimate model for us of how all manner of crosses are born is, of course, Jesus Christ Himself. Christ's actions and words as recorded in the Gospels teach us not only how to cope with suffering but also how to tap into its redemptive power, by "offering up" our sufferings, joining them with Christ's Passion, for the remission of sins and for spiritual benefits for ourselves and for others.

---

[66] Peter Kreeft, *Making Sense Out of Suffering* (Cincinnati: St. Anthony Messenger Press, 1986), 137.

Let us turn now to the loneliness of Jesus Christ on the Cross and on His journey there, so that we can learn His lessons and experience the kind of emotional and spiritual connection with God that can give our own loneliness meaning as we wait for the joys yet to come.

The Profundity and Power of Christ's Loneliness

We can profit by imagining Christ's loneliness on the Cross, as we'll do in our next section, but Christ's loneliness was not limited to those few hours of agony. What loneliness He must have felt beforehand, to know that His execution loomed near, that He would die an early death by the explicit will of His own countrymen (even through the actions of a close friend), that His family and friends could do nothing about it, that they would suffer immensely through the cruelty of His death and from the loss of His companionship on earth! Through the grace of God, we have been given some sublime insights into Christ's loneliness as He awaited His execution. These reflections were provided to us by a great Christian saint and lover of Christ as he faced, in some sense, a similar fate of his own.

I speak of St. Thomas More (1478–1535), the learned, accomplished lawyer who rose to the office of chancellor of England, second in power only to his friend King Henry VIII (1491–1547). From his prison cell in the Tower of London Thomas famously declared exactly where his loyalties resided: "I die the king's faithful servant, but God's first." His crimes included his steadfast refusal, despite desperate entreaties from family and friends, to sign King Henry's declaration that Henry was the Supreme Head of the Church of England. Thomas knew well, after all, that Peter was the rock on whom Christ built His Church (Matt. 16:18) and the popes are Peter's successors. To remain true to Christ and His Church, St. Thomas was willing to forgo his freedom and, in about fifteen months, his life, as he suffered execution. He was sentenced by the court to be hanged, drawn, and quartered, the punishment for treason committed by non-nobles, but his friend King Henry commuted it to beheading.

The relevance of St. Thomas More for us is a book that he wrote in that tower. It is known as *The Sadness of Christ* but was originally entitled *The Sadness, the Weariness, the Fear, and the Prayer of Christ before He Was Taken Prisoner.* St. Thomas's own sufferings gave him insights into the sufferings of Christ — including His loneliness — that might help us join our sufferings to Christ's. In the paragraphs that follow, I draw mostly from St. Thomas's insights but include here and there a few of my own elaborations pertaining to the themes of loneliness and friendship.

St. Thomas dwells at greatest length on Christ's agonizing night of prayer in the garden of Gethsemane at the foot of the Mount of Olives that ended in his betrayal and capture (Matt. 26:36–56; Mark 14:32–52; Luke 22:39–54; John 18:1–12). Jesus, fully man as well as God, was profoundly sad, weary, and fearful that night. He was so distressed as He prayed to His Father that He experienced what physicians call hematohidrosis, sweating blood, when the capillaries that fed His sweat glands burst under His immense mental and physical duress. Christ was not only sad, fatigued, and fearful in the face of His upcoming torments but was also profoundly lonely, although his friends Peter, James, and John were close by, but "a stone's throw" away (Luke 22:41).

Jesus had told His disciples earlier that they would fall away from Him that very night as had been prophesied: "I will strike the shepherd, and the sheep of the flock will be scattered" (Matt. 26:31; cf. Zech. 13:7). Peter boldly declared that although the others might all fall away from Him, he himself would follow Jesus even unto death. Jesus knew this was not the case and told Peter to his dismay that he would deny Him three times that same night before the cock would crow. Yet Peter, James, and John would fall away from Christ a full three times in yet another sense before that cock would crow.

When Jesus arrives at the garden of Gethsemane, He asks the three to sit and watch with Him while He goes off a short distance to pray. He had revealed to his friends that His soul was "very sorrowful, even to death" (Matt. 26:38; Mark 14:34) before He asked them to remain vigilant. When Jesus moves a short distance away, He does not sit, or even kneel, but falls flat on the ground and beseeches His Father to remove the cup of suffering and death before Him, if possible, adding, "not as I will, but as thou wilt" (Matt. 26:39; Mark 14:36; Luke 22:42). Jesus then returns to His disciples and finds all three not vigilant and watching, as He had asked them to be during His time of great need, but already fast asleep. He rouses them, asks Peter if he cannot stay awake even for an hour to watch, and asks them to watch and pray so that they will not "enter into temptation" (Matt. 26:41). Again he prays to his Father, asking if the cup might pass if it is the Father's will, and again He returns to find His friends asleep. He goes off by Himself a third time to repeat the same prayer only to find them again still asleep upon His return. He rouses them and tells them that His hour is at hand, now that His betrayer had arrived.

While Peter, James, and John slept, another friend of Jesus has been wide awake, that friend being his betrayer, Judas Iscariot. He arrives in the garden with a great armed crowd and identifies Jesus with the sign of a kiss. Jesus' first words to Judas, knowing his intentions, were, most poignantly, "Friend, why are you here?" (Matt. 26:50). Jesus still called his betrayer "friend."

We can but imagine Jesus' profound loneliness at this time. Three of His closest friends slept during His time of greatest need, while another friend actively plotted against Him. Judas had been, or at least had postured to be, a virtuous, spiritual friend, seeking holiness with Christ and the other apostles, and yet he debased their friendship, turning it into the most heinous of false and worldly friendships, seeking his own monetary gain even at the cost of the life of his friend.

Jesus' sad and lonely night was not over yet, however. Before the cock crowed to announce the morning, His friend and "Rock" Peter would indeed deny three times that he even knew Him.

This scene opens us to all kinds of personal reflection. Have *you* ever felt sad and lonely when a friend or perhaps even a spouse let you down in your time of need, or worse yet, outright betrayed you? Have you ever *been* the friend who let your spouse or another friend down or betrayed him or her by your actions? Our lesson here from Christ is that His love still goes out to those who let Him down or even betray Him, provided we are willing to ask for forgiveness. Judas, of course, later realized that he had sinned against innocent blood, and he repented of his act and returned his ill-gotten thirty pieces of silver to the priests and elders — before he hanged himself, dying, in fact, before the death of the friend he had betrayed. Centuries later, in the *Dialogues* of St. Catherine of Siena, God revealed to her in a mystical ecstasy that Judas's greatest sin was not that he betrayed Jesus, but that he despaired of God's mercy and willingness to forgive him. We should bear that in mind if we ever feel we might have committed some unpardonable sin against God or against a dear friend here on earth.

St. Thomas More reaps all kinds of spiritual lessons from this scene in the garden, and one more of them certainly merits our attention for the hope with which it can provide the lonely. Thomas considers that some Christian martyrs are known for how they bravely faced death and seemed almost to provoke it or at least to welcome it with open arms. Christ Himself, of course, did eventually go to His Crucifixion for us with literally open arms, and yet the God-Man Himself experienced such anguish and anxiety that He sweat blood (Luke 22:44). Thomas's own profound words about what Christ might have put into words on the matter certainly bear repeating:

> Let the brave man have his high-spirited martyrs, let him rejoice in imitating a thousand of them. But you, my timorous and feeble little sheep, be content to have me alone as your shepherd, follow my leadership; if you do not trust yourself, place your trust in me. See, I am walking ahead of you along this fearful road. Take hold of the border of my garment and you will feel going out from it a power which will stay your heart's blood from issuing vain tears and will make your heart more cheerful, especially when you remember that you are following closely in my footsteps (and I am to be trusted and will not allow you to be tempted beyond what you can bear, but I will give together with the temptation a way out that you may be able to endure it).[67]

[67] St. Thomas More, *The Sadness of Christ* (New York: Scepter Publishers, 1993), 16.

Christ is always there to comfort, console, and strengthen us through all manner of trials, including those of loneliness. We need merely to stay awake and ask Him through prayer, following in His footsteps as He prayed through the night in Gethsemane, grasping His garment, and feeling His power. The Father did not remove His cup but gave Him all the strength He needed to drink from it fully in His Passion. Indeed, even during His prayer in the garden, "there appeared to him an angel of heaven, strengthening him" (Luke 22:43). God and the angels are always there for us too, if we would call upon them.

Christ's Seven Last Words

And now we turn to some of the lessons Christ poured out for us while He drained that cup of suffering for our sakes. St. Augustine brilliantly observed: "The tree upon which were fixed the members of Him dying was even the chair of the Master teaching."[68] St. Thomas Aquinas admirably provides us with one of those lessons that Augustine gleaned from that teaching chair of the Cross. "*Not without purpose did He choose the class of death, that He might be a teacher of that breadth and height, and length, and depth,* of which the Apostle speaks (Eph. 3:18)."[69]

As for the *breadth*, Augustine declares that the crossbeam of the Cross represents *good works*, since Christ's hands were spread out upon it. The *length* of the Cross from the crossbeam to the ground, where it is planted, stands, and abides, represents the virtue of *longanimity*, which bears all things over time. The Cross's *height* from the crossbeam to its top held the head of the

---

[68] Cited by St. Thomas Aquinas in *ST*, III, Q. 45, art. 4.
[69] *ST*, III, Q. 46, art. 1.

crucified Christ, who is the *supreme desire and hope* of believers. Finally, the *depth* of the Cross, hidden in the earth from view, holds it fixed like the root from which the entire tree grows, and this represents the depth of God's *gratuitous grace.*

Of course, Jesus taught us not only metaphorically through the wood of the Cross but also through the words that He spoke from that most painful teaching chair. For centuries Catholics have pondered the rich meaning of Jesus' seven last words from the Cross. These "words" are the seven brief sayings Jesus uttered while He hung on the Cross in utmost pain and loneliness. Let's look at them, consider their Source and their context, and ponder how they might console and strengthen us as we bear our own immeasurably lighter crosses.

1. "Father, forgive them, for they know
not what they do." (Luke 23:34)
Christ's first words from the Cross, in the earliest throes of His agony, are to ask God to forgive the very people who placed Him there. How many of us are lonely because of estrangement from someone once close to us whom we have refused to forgive or who has been unforgiving of us? Can we make a gesture to reach out to that person while our arms remain free to move? Even if we should be rebuffed, can we do as Christ did and pray that God will forgive that person—and us, too?

2. "Truly, I say to you, today you will be
with me in Paradise." (Luke 23:43)
The completely innocent Christ was given two criminals as His companions as He hung from the Cross. One of them railed at Him, demanding that He save them all if He truly was the Christ. The other rebuked the first for not fearing God present

in Christ, who suffered the same punishment as theirs even though He was innocent. When that "good thief" asked Jesus to remember him when He came into His kingly power, Jesus uttered His second word from the Cross: "Truly, I say to you, today you will be with me in Paradise." These words certainly brought that thief incredible solace and joy. If we are or should become victims of severe emotional or social isolation, how might we treat those in the same boat, bearing a similar cross? Will we recognize Christ in them and treat them accordingly? Our ultimate reward will be great one day should we, too, share Paradise with Christ.

3. *"Woman, behold, your son. . . .*
Behold, your mother." (John 19:26–27)
Now imagine Christ's loneliness as He looks down at His totally loving, devoted, and sinless mother, beside John, His "beloved disciple." He knows how they share His tortures and will soon have to cope with His loss in their earthly existence, but He is anything but paralyzed by His distress. He wants those whom He loves to continue to love and care for each other in the most intimate of ways, as that between a mother and her child, a child and his mother. Of course, Jesus grants Mary as Queen of Heaven to be mother not only to John but to every man and woman on earth. She is as willing to fly to our aid today as she was to John's on the day of Christ's Crucifixion.

Centuries after that day, St. Thérèse of Lisieux would ponder the strength of the Blessed Mother in enduring so many sorrows, noting that, unlike all of us, Mary herself did not have a Blessed Mother to pray to (although, of course, she had her Son)! So, is there a lonely person in your life, perhaps someone bereaved of a parent, or a child, for whom you might step forward and offer love and support, as John and the Blessed Mother offered each other love and support?

4. *"My God, my God, why hast thou forsaken me?" (Matt. 27:46; Mark 15:34)*

Christ here echoes Psalm 22:1, which expresses the desolation He felt in His human nature. Here is Christ suffering. Here is another example of how we can join our suffering with Christ's. In our loneliest hours, do we feel that we are forsaken not only by man, but by God? If so, can we still call out to God in prayer, expecting that He will hear us?

5. *"I thirst." (John 19:28)*

Here is another reminder that Christ joined us in our humanity. The eternal Word who was in the beginning, who was with God, and who was God (see John 1:1) has agreed to take on the weakness, the cravings, and the gnawing of the human flesh of His creatures, for our own sake, and yet we let Him suffer. Do we take much time to think of the lonely people in our lives for whom Christ died and of how they might thirst for attention? And we needn't get too metaphorical, for sometimes the lonely are isolated and may experience physical thirst and hunger that we might help relieve. The Church has always recognized that we are not disembodied souls, but ensouled bodies and both elements of our unity are good and deserving of care. This is why she has long encouraged both spiritual and corporal (fleshly, bodily) works of mercy.

In fact, sometimes we spend so much time in the virtual, electronic world that we forget that we all have bodies with needs we can help each other fulfill. When a text or an e-mail replaces a phone call, we have cut ourselves off from the recipient's voice.

When a call replaces face-to-face contact, we have cut ourselves off not only from that person's face, but from his or her body language, all those subtle ways that God has given us to communicate with one another by virtue of having bodies. When we connect only over distant airwaves, we can certainly suggest that a thirsty friend get a drink, but we are in no position to hand him one.

6. "It is finished." (John 19:30)

What a relief Christ must have felt when His task, the most gruesome yet important task ever assigned on earth, was complete! He expressed it in these simple words: "It is finished." Our own life task is clearly not finished. What, then, will we do to establish new emotional and social connections and strengthen the ones we already have in our time left on earth before, God willing, we pass through the gates of heaven Christ opened for us by completing His mission on the wood of the Cross?

7. "Father, into thy hands I commit my spirit!" (Luke 23:46)

These are the very last words Jesus breathed on earth before His spirit returned to His Father. Will our focus be on God in our last moment? It is, after all, "in Him that we live and move and have our being" (Acts 17:28). Are we willing to commit our spirits to God *now*? Such commitment to God, who is no mere abstract power or force, let alone an uncaring ruler, but is our Father, who has given His Son for our salvation, and who gives us His Holy Spirit to dwell in the temples of our bodies, cannot help but provide relief to our deepest feelings of loneliness, and motivation to reach out with His love to the lonely around us.

This chapter too is finished, but before moving on to the next, let's take a moment to meditate just a bit on Jesus in the garden and upon the Cross. Let's ask ourselves how we might unite our sufferings with Christ's and, despite what may befall us, resolve to trust in Him and commit our spirits to the Father's loving hands.

Action Plan

Read. Read the Gospel accounts of Christ's night of prayer in the Garden of Gethsemane and the deep loneliness He experienced even though his friends were nearby (Matt. 26:36–56; Mark 14:32–52; Luke 22:39–54). Also read Matthew 27, Mark 15, Luke 23, and John 19 with special attention to Jesus' seven last words on the Cross. If possible, do your reading in front of a crucifix, to be mindful of Christ on His "teaching chair" of the Cross. Finally, read St. Thomas More's *The Sadness of Christ* to meditate more deeply upon the loneliness Christ took on for us.

Reflect. The next time you suffer from loneliness, unite your suffering with Christ's and offer it up to God. Suffering, when offered up to God, like Christ's, can eventually yield great blessings. There would have been no Resurrection without the Passion.

Remember. Can you think back to difficult times in your life that you would not now trade for the world? Remember that suffering can truly make us stronger, more patient, enduring, and compassionate toward the suffering of others. If you have borne the burden of severe loneliness, perhaps through bereavement, let it remind you that others have been and are bearing their own pains of loneliness, and think of things you can do to help them endure and grow from it.

Recite. Pray that God will give you strength in your loneliest hour. Pray the prayer that Christ gave us. As He cried out, "Father," from the Cross, so, too, did He teach us to start our prayer with "Our Father."

Reconnect. Even while pinioned upon the Cross, Christ reached out and connected to others—with the "good thief" and with His mother and His beloved disciple. Let this remind you that you, too, can reach out in loving ways both to strangers and to family and friends even at times when you might feel immobilized by loneliness.

Recent Loneliness Studies
Make the Headlines

In 2006, the *American Sociological Review* created quite a stir when it released the results of a twenty-year study from the University of Chicago comparing surveys of two samples of approximately 1,500 adults each, the first taken in 1985 and the second in 2004.[70] The accompanying table (see next page) provides a summary of a few of the key findings regarding intimate relationships of close confidants, the lack of which can contribute to the loneliness of emotional isolation.

The researchers reported that "in spite of a large literature on declining civic engagement and neighbor involvement" (e.g., recall Putnam's *Bowling Alone*), they expected that networks of close confidants would have remained stable. When the updated survey results came in, the researchers stated quite bluntly: "We were clearly wrong." So striking were these findings that, shortly after, articles appeared in popular periodicals such as *USA Today*, the *New York Times*, and the *American Spectator*, and many others, some headlining with some variant of the startling finding that "One-quarter of Americans have no one to confide in!"

[70] Miller McPherson, Lynn Smith-Lovin, and Matthew E. Brashears, "Social Isolation in America: Changes in Core Discussion Networks over Two Decades," *American Sociological Review* 71 (June 2006): 353–375.

Modern Research Reveals an

National Opinion Survey Year	1985	2004
Average number of people one can confide in about important matters	3	2
Modal number of confidants (Of a range of 0 to 6 or more close confidants, the modal number is the number of confidants reported by the greatest number of respondents. By 2004 more people reported they had no close confidants than those who reported either 1, 2, 3, 4, 5, or 6+ confidants, while 3 confidants was the most common response two decades before.)	3	0
People with no close confidants	10%	25%
People who mentioned a sibling as confidant	21%	14%
People who mentioned a parent as confidant	23%	21%

American Culture of Loneliness

National Opinion Survey Year	1985	2004
People who mentioned a child as confidant	18%	10%
People who mentioned a friend as confidant	73%	51%
People who mentioned a neighbor as confidant	19%	8%
People who mentioned a coworker as confidant	29%	12%
People who mentioned spouse as confidant	30%	38%
People who confide only in family members	57%	80%
People who confide only in their spouses	5%	9%

The researchers concluded: "The data may overestimate the number of social isolates, but these shrinking networks reflect an important social change in America."[71]

In 2010, the American Association of Retired People (AARP) published an extensive report entitled *Loneliness among Older Adults: A National Survey of Adults 45+*.[72] About one-third (35 percent) of their more than 3,000 respondents reported significant loneliness with no significant difference between men (37 percent) and women (34 percent). Perhaps not surprisingly, the AARP's study showed that the fewer confidants a person reported, the more likely he or she was to be lonely.

Recent studies have estimated that up to 32 percent of adults experience loneliness, and up to 7 percent describe intense feelings of loneliness. To get some sense of the magnitude of those percentages, with the current (2017) U.S. population of more than 326 million people, about 142 million may be lonely, and about 23 million may be lonely to an intense degree—truly a vast number of suffering souls.

In 2013 the *Journal of Psychology* devoted issues 1 and 2 of its volume 146 entirely to articles on loneliness.[73]

[71] McPherson, Smith-Lovin, and Brashears, "Social Isolation," 353.

[72] Interested readers can find it online at https://assets.aarp.org/rgcenter/general/loneliness_2010.pdf.

[73] Ami Rokach, ed., *Loneliness Updated: Recent Research on Loneliness and How It Affects Our Lives* (New York: Routledge, 2013).

The issues' editor, psychologist Ami Rokach, provided a powerful, insightful personal observation about loneliness. In thirty years of teaching and presenting about loneliness, whenever he has asked students or audience members if there is anyone who has *never* experienced loneliness, no hands go up, and whenever he asks if anyone is experiencing loneliness *now*, not a single person has ever raised a hand to admit it. He argues that loneliness carries a social stigma. People seem to think that admitting to loneliness bespeaks a lack of meaningful friendships and other social ties and implies personal inadequacies or socially undesirable traits. How sad that the pain of emotional and social isolation is often compounded by negative thoughts about oneself.

The dozens of researchers who contributed to the *Journal of Psychology* special issues in 2013 looked at loneliness from a great many angles, from children and teens who are left home alone, to elderly Appalachians with health-care issues, to elderly Israelis cared for by foreign caretakers who could not communicate with them in their own language.

Hardly two years after those special issues devoted to loneliness, *Perspectives on Psychological Science* ran a special section with a handful of studies on loneliness in its March 2015 edition. Topics included the genetic factors involved in loneliness, the clinical importance of loneliness, loneliness's impact on mortality, and ways to intervene to overcome loneliness.

Suffice it to say that the once relatively ignored subject of loneliness is clearly among the most important subjects of interest and concern to social scientists and medical practitioners in our time. Anyone at any age anywhere around the world can be subject to loneliness, and the numbers are clearly climbing. Every one of us should ask God, and ask ourselves, what we can do to stem this tide of loneliness. In the next chapter, we'll examine a few possible answers.

Chapter 6

Lightening the Burden of Our Neighbor's Loneliness

We love because he first loved us. If anyone says, "I love
God," and hates his brother, he is a liar; for he who does not
love his brother whom he has seen, cannot love God whom
he has not seen. And this commandment we have from
him, that he who loves God should love his brother also.

—1 John 4:19–21

"Lord, when did we see thee hungry or thirsty or a stranger or
naked or sick or in prison and we did not minister to thee?"
Then he will answer them, "Truly I say to you, as you did
it not to one of the least of these, you did it not to me."

—Matthew 25:44–45

Turn thou to me and be gracious to me:
for I am lonely and afflicted.

—Psalm 25:16

Sounding the Alarm for a Greater Awakening

In his quest for ways in which we might become more reconnected and invest in "social capital," Robert Putnam argued in the year 2000, "It is hard to see how we could redress the erosion of the last several decades without a major religious contribution."[74] Indeed, he would go on to issue a challenge:

> I challenge America's clergy, lay leaders, theologians, and ordinary worshippers: Let us spur a new, pluralistic, socially responsible "great awakening," so that by 2010 Americans will be more deeply engaged than we are today in one or another spiritual community of meaning, while at the same time becoming more tolerant of the faiths and practices of other Americans.[75]

He then described times in America's history that historians and sociologists have called "awakenings." For example, the first "Great Awakening" of about 1730 to 1760 was inspired by traveling preachers who, in their great revival meetings, drew enormous crowds of people to faith. A similar "Second Great Awakening" occurred from 1800 to 1830 with circuit riders, who

[74] Putnam, *Bowling Alone*, 408–409.
[75] Ibid., 409.

carried the gospel to churches on the western frontier. Putnam noted that their preaching contributed to social movements such as the eventual rejection of slavery and the growth of the Sunday school movement. Some have argued that the move within Protestantism from membership in older mainline denominations to newer evangelical churches in the late 1960s and the early 1970s was another such awakening, as may be the even more recent growth of independent megachurches.

Although such awakenings may indeed have helped forge bonds between Americans and bonds with God, there are certainly some limitations. Psychiatrists (and spouses) Jacqueline Olds and Richard Schwartz express concern that America's primarily Protestant culture can overemphasize self-reliance and underemphasize the need for interpersonal connection. They cite sociologist Robert Bellah, who warned of "the near exclusive focus on the relationship between Jesus and the individual, where accepting Jesus Christ as one's personal Lord and Savior becomes almost the whole of piety."[76] Further, based on interviews he conducted, Bellah noted: "If I may trace the downward spiral of this particular Protestant distortion, let me say that it begins with the statement, 'If I'm all right with Jesus, then I don't need the church.'"[77]

These points are not made to denigrate views held by some Protestants (and perhaps by some Catholics as well), but to point out that if we are to truly to become "awakened" as Christians, we will awaken to each other's needs, including needs for community and interpersonal connections.

[76] Olds and Schwartz, "The Lonely American," 37.
[77] Ibid.

Indeed, if we journey back five hundred years and across the Atlantic Ocean to visit one last time St. Thomas More in his cell, we'll find that the theme he emphasized most is that of the Agony in the Garden, where Jesus repeatedly called to His friends to *wake up* and not sleep during His time of need. Of course, Jesus also told us most clearly that we serve His needs when we love our brother and serve those who thirst, who are strangers, who have not proper clothes to wear, who have become imprisoned, indeed, the least of such living human beings on earth. Only then have we loved and served Jesus. What, then, might Catholics, indeed all Christians, do to wake up and better love and serve the lonely among us in Christ's name? Let me count the ways.

Thirty Ways to Love Your Brother

I imagine that those old enough will recall the popular 1970s song "Fifty Ways to Leave Your Lover." Although the lyrics are not the most charitable (e.g., "Hop on the bus, Gus. You don't need to discuss much. Just drop off the key, Lee, and get yourself free"), they were certainly memorable. And perhaps we can put at least the "fifty ways" idea to some good use here, although I'll pare it down to thirty ways. (Indeed, in the song's lyrics, I count only *five* ways!)

We've covered a lot of ground as we've examined the nature, the causes, and the potential remedies for loneliness from a variety of secular and religious perspectives. If you're still by my side on this journey into and out of loneliness, I'm sure your interest is not merely academic. You are lonely, you have been, or you will be, and the same goes for the people you love. What we seek are things we can do about it, actions we can take that will make a difference for ourselves and our neighbors.

So, in this chapter, I'd like to reiterate some remedies we've considered and offer yet a few more.

St. Thérèse of Lisieux made famous her "little way" of loving God through the simplest daily acts done for her neighbor. I'm sure there are at least thirty little ways to help combat loneliness through simple acts of love for our brothers and sisters. I'll admit, too, that I was briefly tempted to mimic that old song's lyrical style in my recommendations: ("Just smile and say hi, Ty. You can do it if you try, guy." "Help someone onto the bus, Gus, you don't need to be a cuss" ...). After all, St. Thomas Aquinas did tell us that part of being affable, open, and friendly to others is not to be serious all the time, but to exercise "moderate mirth." Alas, I soon saw that such an approach would likely exceed the bounds of moderation and possibly overburden the patience I've encouraged you to build, so I will not do that to you (Lou)! Yet, as a student of memory, I acknowledge the power of rhyme as a potential memory aid, and we are not very likely to perform good deeds that we cannot remember! So then, you'll find some rhymes in the following list, but only in the first word, I insist. Not sure what I mean (Jean)? Then just wait and see (Lee), and try to help another soul get free — from loneliness.

Here we go, then, with thirty little actions you can take to alleviate your own or another's loneliness. Perhaps some of these will strike a chord with you, and perhaps you can think of others of your own.

1. Say

Say to yourself at the start of each day some modification of the wise counsel of Marcus Aurelius, such as the following: "Today I will encounter some lonely person, the bereaved perhaps, the newcomer to this city or to this school or place of work, the person who feels left out even within his own family. This person may ignore me, not look me in the eye, not return my greeting, or treat me with suspicion, but I will remember that such people are my brothers and sisters in Christ and God has called us to be there for one another. Therefore, I will make some effort to connect with this person even in the smallest way to lighten the burden of his loneliness."

2. *Pray*
Pray each day for God's mercy on the lonely, and that He might lighten your burden of separation and help you lighten the burden of others.

3. *Display*
Display the fact that you are aware of other people's presence if you happen to be in the same small space, perhaps in an elevator or a grocery line, with acts as simple as a look in the eye or a nod of your head to acknowledge their human dignity.

4. *Play*
Even the wisest Stoic philosophers, although sometimes popularly portrayed as Spock-like men devoid of emotions, knew the value of play to bring people together, within and across generations. Hear old Epictetus: "When children come up to us and clap their hands and say, 'This is the good Saturnalia,' do we say to them, 'The Saturnalia are not good'? By no means: we clap our hands also" (*Discourses*, I.29). "Who is not tempted by bright and attractive children to join us with their games, and crawl around with them, and talk baby talk with them?" (*Discourses* II.24).

5. *Smile*

What an extremely simple way to show other people they matter to you! If a person is down and lonely, such a simple gesture may be worth far more than it costs you.

6. *Reconcile*

How many people are lonely because of some old grudge they bear that isolates them from formerly close friends or relatives? Remember Christ's words: "So, if you are offering your gift before the altar, and there remember your brother has something against you, leave your gift there before the altar and go; first be reconciled to your brother, and then come and offer your gift" (Matt. 5:23–24). We Catholics also have the great gift of the *sacrament* of reconciliation available to us. Might we examine our conscience for possible sins of commission, or perhaps more likely omission, regarding the needs of the lonely in our lives?

7. *Greet*

Greet loved ones with enthusiasm. How easy it is to take for granted the people who are closest to us, but doing so might contribute to their loneliness even while in our presence.

8. *Eat*

Sharing a meal together is one of the oldest and most meaningful ways of nourishing human connections. It was at the Last Supper that the beloved disciple reclined on Jesus' breast as He gave us the first of countless suppers we would share together at Mass in the Eucharistic celebration. Many faithful Catholics would not miss getting together to share the holy sacrifice of the Eucharist at Mass weekly, if not daily. I wonder how many of them regularly eat together as families in their own home. I know from my own experience and from those of other men in Catholic men's groups that the reestablishment of family meals, during which everyone eats and talks together without electronic intrusions, can go a long way toward rebuilding emotional connections within own home.

9. *Please*

In our selfish times, people often look down on "people pleasers" as weak and foolish since, of course, we should all "look out for number one." And at what great interpersonal loss! Mitchell Kalpakgian, a gracious man I once had the pleasure to share a meal with, speaks of an "art of pleasing" among "the lost arts of modern civilization." He observes: "One of the marks of refinement, civility, and graciousness is the willingness to bring joy into human lives by gratuitous acts of special kindness that respect the wishes or feelings of others—the art of pleasing. The peacefulness of family life, the enjoyment of friends, the harmony of marriage rests upon this art, a skill that attunes persons to the particular preferences and individual sensibilities of others' personalities."[78] How could our loneliness epidemic persist in a world full of civilized people pleasers? What might we do to master this art?

10. *Ease*

In part, Christ's burden is easy and His yoke is light because He has instructed us to share each other's load. Indeed, St. Aelred would write that Christ's yoke is light because it is a yoke of charity. As an unrepentant weightlifter and a fan of strength sports,

---

[78] Mitchell Kalpakgian, *The Lost Arts of Modern Civilization* (Long Prairie, MN: Neumann Press, 2009), 65–66.

I delight in striving to lift ever-heavier physical burdens and in watching those who can lift far more than I can. Still, even in this sport, in which men strive to master the heaviest of loads to outdo one another, I was recently surprised to find that there exist two-man team strength events. It seems that at times, then, even the strongest of men can get by with a little help from their friends (in pulling semitrucks and such)! What, then, might we do to lessen both the physical and mental burdens of those who might need us? How might we build our spiritual strength by looking for and meeting our brothers' needs, so that we, too, might say, like the boy in Father Flanagan's Boys Town, "He ain't heavy, he's my brother"?

11. Write

Letter writing is another of Mitchell Kalpakgian's "lost arts." When was the last time you wrote or received a letter? Of course, in our day of instant messaging, texting, and e-mailing, few people are likely to return fully to the cost and delays of old-fashioned snail mail. Again, though, at what loss? Not only does writing a letter show that writer has devoted time and attention to the recipient, but a personal letter also bears the mark of the writer in the form of his unique handwriting and signature. (I understand that in some school districts students are not even taught how to write or read cursive anymore.) Still, even if we might not return fully to letter writing, can we train ourselves to grace every card we send with at least a little personal hand-written note? (Whenever my family sends a card, every one of us signs it individually to show that we all care enough for the recipient to take the time to do so.) Further, once in a while, even in our home, we can certainly grab a Post-it note or a random slip of paper, write a note, and plant it somewhere to surprise our spouse or another loved one and let that person know that we're thinking of him or her.

12. Invite

If you are lonely or know someone who is, take the risk of inviting that person, or someone new, to join you in some simple activity, such as having lunch at your office or school, taking a walk around the building during a break, or attending a church men's or women's group with you.

13. Reunite

More than forty years ago, I was blessed to graduate from a small Catholic grade school that still has informal reunions every few years. As I write, I await what I'm billing as the "Olde-Tyme Strongman Get Together" next weekend at my home, where a handful or more of my old-time powerlifting team buddies from the early 1980s will get together with our spouses to reminisce (and to make sure that everybody is still lifting!). Is there some group of people you were close to at some time in your life — old classmates, teammates, or workmates perhaps — whom you might try to reunite with and maybe reestablish old bonds? They might just be waiting for your call.

14. Show insight

In a warm, wonderful book, Fr. Lawrence Lovasik makes clear a key element of mastering the art of pleasing others and making important connections: "If you are a person of gentle feelings, you will attract others by a certain delicacy and attention to their small needs, by discovering their least desires and constantly forgoing your own, and by rendering little services even before they are requested. Do not wait for your neighbor to express a wish, but gratify his unspoken wish. Keep your eyes open to other's needs."[79] Christ, after all, told us to be proactive and "*do unto* others," not merely to wait and *respond* to them.

15. Be polite
Cultivate the habit of showing courtesy, consideration, and respect to every person you meet. Nothing will open doors quite like it, and while we're on the subject, holding doors for others is one simple example. Who likes to have a door slam in his face, as if he did not exist? Imagine how this might feel to a person struggling with severe loneliness.

16. Delight!
Mitchell Kalpakgian writes of simply "enjoying people" as among the lost arts of modern civilization, which, of course, caught my attention when he opened his chapter with a quotation from St. Thomas Aquinas: "No man can live without pleasure." There are real and ominous signs of decline in this art, and at civilization's peril. Kalpakgian notes: "The decline in population in Western Europe and America is one symptom of this loss of enjoyment in people, of the delight in children. In a culture in which a society is not replacing itself, the enjoyment of children as one of life's greatest sources of happiness holds no privileged place in the hierarchy of pleasures."[80] Perhaps surprisingly, decades before, even the great atheist philosopher Bertrand Russell had

---

[79] Fr. Lawrence G. Lovasik, *The Hidden Power of Kindness: A Practical Handbook for Souls Who Dare to Transform the World, One Deed at a Time* (Manchester, NH: Sophia Institute Press, 1999), 8.
[80] Kalpakgian, Lost Arts, 50.

warned of this trend: "Those whose outlook on life causes them to feel so little happiness that they do not care to beget children are biologically doomed. Before long they must be succeeded by something gayer and jollier!"[81] May we do our part to bring a jollier existence to the lonely, with special attention to the needs and joys of children.

17. Ask

One way to connect with strangers and to help relieve their loneliness is to show them they are valuable and needed by you. In his intriguing autobiography, the crafty Founding Father Benjamin Franklin reported that when he sought out a new friendship with someone, rather than trying to do him some favor to win his goodwill, he would sometimes instead *ask a favor of that person*, perhaps the loan of a rare book he had heard that the person had. In that way, he also indirectly did the person a favor by giving him the opportunity to be generous and helpful. Thus, by asking another for some small favor, you might open the door to a new meaningful connection. Indeed, modern psychiatrists and loneliness experts Jacqueline Olds and Richard Schwartz suggest that a return to habits of old as simple as asking a neighbor to borrow a cup of sugar rather than hopping in the car and driving to the store might help end the lonely isolation of so many modern neighborhoods.

18. Task

A commonsense recommendation for the lonely is to join some kind of group. This is sound advice, but some kinds of groups

---

[81] Bertrand Russell, *The Conquest of Happiness* (New York: W. W. Norton, 1996), 54.

may be more likely to foster meaningful relationships than others. For example, while some lonely people looking for romantic relationships do indeed find their mates through Internet sites (including Catholic ones) specifically set up for facilitating such connections, other lonely people may find it daunting to offer their profile for public inspection and scrutiny. Such hesitations could be addressed with the rational thinking methods of cognitive therapy, but another alternative is to seek out groups whose focus is not directly on forming relationships but on jointly pursuing some external task, such as church groups or groups formed to foster some cause or to enjoy some hobby. As psychiatrists Olds and Schwartz have opined: "We believe that when two or more people are involved in a shared task, their interaction forms an ongoing context. Furthermore, it is only within such a context that relationships can deepen."[82]

19. Think

If you are lonely, don't forget that you can work to catch your automatic thoughts and modify your thinking when you become especially distressed or immobilized by loneliness and feel unable to take the kinds of actions that might help you overcome it. If you find that your efforts are unsuccessful after repeated attempts, consider seeking therapy through a counselor who can help you learn to think more adaptively. Further, part of the effectiveness of therapy in remitting loneliness is the relationship that forms between the therapist and the client. In fact, Olds, Schwartz, and Webster consider therapy a clear-cut example of the kind of

---

[82] Jacqueline Olds, Richard Schwartz, and Harriet Webster, *Overcoming Loneliness in Everyday Life* (New York: Birch Lane Press, 1996), 58.

shared task through which intimacy grows. Still, they emphasize that the relationship and support developed in therapy should not take the place of other normal human relationships but should inspire and equip us to form, nurture, and cherish them. As Catholics, we might also seek a spiritual director who can help us draw closer to God and better cope with or offer up the sorrows of loneliness.

20. Thank

Especially if you are lonely due to the loss of a loved one, cultivate the habit of thanking God for the time you and that person had together on earth as you hope for a reunion in heaven. Epictetus gave interesting and worthwhile advice in this regard, knowing full well that it is not easy to follow: "Never say about anything, 'I have lost it,' but instead, 'I have given it back.' Did your child die? It was given back. Did your wife die? She was given back.... As long as he (God, the Giver), gives it, take care of it as something that is not your own, just as travelers treat an inn."[83] As Christians, we know that everyone dear in our life for any time is truly a gift from God. We know, too, that we, like they, are wayfarers here on earth, and one day our loved ones will have to give us back to the loving Giver.

21. Thunk

Sorry, but I couldn't resist using this nonstandard past tense of *think*. Here I'd like to remind you of the proper kind of social thinking skills that can help to alleviate loneliness applied not to current stresses and situations as much as to those in the past. Recall that research has shown that loneliness can make

---

[83] *Handbook of Epictetus*, 14.

for a kind of selective memory in which the lonely are much more likely to remember negative than positive past interactions with others. When we are lonely, then, we need to examine ourselves for this tendency to see the world with the opposite of rose-colored glasses. Also, when interacting with lonely people, we need to keep this tendency in mind and be patient if they misinterpret our gestures to reach out to them.

22. Admit

Admit you are lonely if you truly are. One of the most serious concerns in health-care professions about the rising epidemic of loneliness is that due to its stigma, few people report it, and what is not reported is not likely to be treated and relieved. Indeed, as Robert Weiss pointed out decades ago, even among doctors and therapists who have felt lonely, there is a tendency when looking back at periods of loneliness to think, "But I wasn't myself then" and to forget the distress one experienced. "As an implication, we might expect that those who are not at the moment lonely will have little empathy for those who are, even if in the recent past they had been lonely themselves."[84] So, those who are currently lonely ought to admit it, while those of us not lonely right now ought to ratchet up our awareness of and empathy for the loneliness of others, by reflecting at times about past periods of loneliness in our own lives.

23. Submit

As Catholics, we have at our disposal all sorts of aids from above that can help us cope with, overcome, and help others through

[84] Robert S. Weiss, *Loneliness: The Experience of Emotional and Social Isolation*, (Cambridge, MA: MIT Press, 1973), 11.

loneliness. The ones I speak of here require only that we submit to the stirrings of the Holy Spirit within us. Fear of the Lord, piety, knowledge, fortitude, counsel, understanding, and wisdom (Isa. 11:2–3; CCC 1831) are given to us in Baptism and strengthened in Confirmation. As human virtues perfect our powers to act as guided by our reason, these supernatural gifts perfect the virtues themselves, making us amenable not merely to the workings of our limited reason but to the stirrings or motions of the Holy Spirit in our souls. Submitting our wills to the Holy Spirit to accept, learn about, and employ these supernatural gifts is itself to establish a relationship with God that can help overcome feelings of isolation.

24. Slow

Slow down the pace of your life. Olds and Schwartz observe a vicious cycle common to many Americans: the cycle of busyness. Husbands and wives are commonly both working full-time now, perhaps also working overtime and additional part-time jobs, and taking the fewest number of vacation days throughout the world. We are busy to obtain the money to acquire many material things and for some, busyness itself has become a status symbol. After all, we must be very important if we are constantly busy! This busyness can erode social relationships when time spent socializing is seen as time wasted. Further, being so busy that we rarely have time to call on our friends sends them the message that they are not important to us, making it less likely that they will reach out to us either.

25. Go

Go ahead, though, and do try to reinitiate those little calls and visits that matter if you believe this scenario applies to you.

Sometimes people are hesitant to reach out again when they get the "Aha!" experience that they have seriously neglected a friend. "Will he [or she] even want to hear from me now?" There is only one way to find out for sure.

26. Listen

Listen to others, just as Simon, I mean Sirach, says: "If you love to listen, you will gain knowledge; and if you incline your ear, you will become wise" (Sir. 6:33). Even loved ones close to you may feel lonely in your presence if you do not take the time to listen to what they have to say. I recall reading Mortimer Adler's observation in *How to Speak: How to Listen* that listening is not a passive but an active process, wherein we need to work to focus our attention. How easy it is to be so engrossed in our own concerns and interests that we spend our listening part of the conversation just preparing for what we are going to say next—that is, if we grant our partner in conversation a listening part at all. A good rule of thumb for the overly talkative to keep in mind is that if we are conversing with one other person, we should not spend more than about one-half of the time in speaking.

27. Glisten

Forgive me if "glisten" is a bit of a stretch, but I hark back to the old saying expressing perhaps an overly delicate etiquette: "Horses sweat; men perspire; women glisten." I really am talking about plain old sweat in the sense that the ancient poet Hesiod put it: "To achieve excellence, we first must sweat." This phrase certainly applies to athletics, but also to so much more, for in ancient Greek the word *arête* (excellence) was also their word for "virtue," since virtues are excellences of the soul. Here, though, I'll get back to the physical body and actual glistening sweat! We are all called to take proper care of our bodies within our physical capacities, and all kinds of exercise and sports provide nearly ideal opportunities to share common tasks with other people that can forge strong bonds of relationships and friendships. Indeed, many of my closest friends over the years have been people I met in the gym. Sure, at first we bonded based on the pleasure we took in weight lifting, and the usefulness we provided one another, as in spotting one another and sharing our knowledge of lifting techniques and routines, but many did blossom into friendships of virtue — the virtues of fitness, at least![85] Indeed, I met my wife of thirty-two years and counting at the gym as well. So, if you are seeking some new interpersonal connections, consider joining a fitness center, a golf club, a tennis club … what do they call that new game? — yes, "pickle ball." What about running, card playing, or any kind of local group that caters to an interest you have or one you might like to develop? As a side note, too, I'll point out that from years of experience working out and working in the fitness-center business, different regular groups of people usually come in religiously at different times of the day, from the early risers in the wee hours, to the "silver sneakers" crowd of retirees who tend to favor the midmorning hours, making way for noon-hour workers (perhaps a bit rushed for too much socializing), to the after-work crowd and even the night owls. If you don't feel you connect with the crowd at one time, go at another time, and you might feel much more at home and acquire a new batch of training buddies who might enjoy "chewing the fat" with you as much as burning it.

---

[85] As St. Thomas once wisely observed: "Virtue, inasmuch as it is a suitable disposition of the soul, is like health and beauty, which are suitable dispositions of the body." *ST*, I-II, Q. 55, art. 2.

28. Use

Use social media wisely. Don't let your Facebook friends replace the friends you can see face-to-face. Use social media to create new bonds or reestablish old ones with people too far away for you to see in person and as a means of keeping connected to friends who are nearby by doing things such as inviting them to events and activities where you can meet. If your use of social media has become too time consuming and bordering on addiction, consider setting an egg timer by your computer or smartphone to limit how long you will sit there like an egg before you move from the virtual world back into the real three-dimensional one.

29. Abuse

Abuse television no more! I saw a commercial just last night (yes, while watching TV) that encouraged viewers to have a television connected in every room of the house. Is that the kind of connection you'd like to encourage in your home? Even decades ago, research showed that "as the number of TV sets per household multiplies, even watching television together becomes rarer."[86] While TV has played a large role in our increasing isolation, that does not mean that it must continue to do so. This does not necessarily mean we should chuck all TVs out the window. After all, entertaining, educational, and inspirational programs and channels do exist, and only God knows how many souls have been brought to Christ and the community of His Catholic Church through wonderful Catholic programming. Perhaps to use rather than abuse our televisions,

[86] Putnam, *Bowling Alone*, 224.

we can simply take the time to plan ahead what we will watch, whom we will watch it with, and how long we will watch it.[87] Even Robert Putnam's research on the powerful impact of TV showed that the greatest risk to reduced social activity was found for those in the habit of aimless channel surfing, rather than those who turned on the TV only when they had some particular program in mind to view.

30. Choose

Choose the good portion. You'll recall that when Jesus visited with Mary and Martha, Mary sat at His feet and listened to His teaching, while Martha scurried about, distractedly serving things to the guests. When Martha asked Jesus to tell Mary to help her, He replied: "Martha, Martha, you are anxious and troubled about many things; one thing is needful. Mary has chosen the good portion, which will not be taken away from her" (Luke 10:41–42). To obtain the good portion, we must not be so distracted by all the cares, the troubles, and the perpetual calls to a trivial busyness in the world that we do not see Christ sitting there right under our noses, hoping that we will see Him and listen to Him, whether He sits there clothed in the earthly body that Martha saw that day or in the bodies of our neighbors who are with us every day.

---

[87] Putnam's research review indicated that the average American watched about 4 hours of TV per day at the turn of the millennium. Statistics from 2016 put it at 4.3 hours, and this in addition to time spent on the Internet. Some recent sources estimate that we now spend up to 8 or 9 hours per day connected to some form of media. St. Paul advised us to "pray constantly," not to be prey of the media constantly!

Action Plan

As we come to the end of this book we've seen action plans aplenty (not to mention the thirty practical suggestions within this chapter). For this last action plan, then, I'll ask you to take action and complete an action plan of your own design to reach out to the lonely people in your life and to help foster a culture of care and connectedness. As for the "Read" section, I'll give you a bit of a head start by noting that I've mentioned a few good books on reaching out to others and combating the culture of loneliness in the text and the footnotes of this chapter. Perhaps one of those intrigued you. If not, what reading can you think of that might motivate you to help alleviate loneliness? The heartfelt psalms of David? *The Imitation of Christ* or a favorite devotional? Perhaps something else? As for the rest, I'll leave them up to you and thank you for doing your part to make this a less lonely world through, with, and in Jesus Christ.

Read.

Reflect.

Remember.

Recite.

Reconnect.

The Rise of the Machines

Real relationships with others, with all the challenges they entail, now tend to be replaced by a type of internet communication which enables us to choose or eliminate relationships at whim, thus giving rise to a new type of contrived emotion which has more to do with devices and displays than with other people and with nature. Today's media do enable us to communicate and to share our knowledge and affections. Yet at times they also shield us from direct contact with the pain, the fears and the joys of others and the complexity of their personal experiences. For this reason, we should be concerned that, alongside the exciting possibilities offered by these media, a deep and melancholic dissatisfaction with interpersonal relations, or a harmful sense of isolation, can also arise.

—Pope Francis, *Laudato Si'*, no. 47

During the same recent decades in which we've seen unparalleled advances in technology, we've also seen *decreases* in reported levels of happiness, along with *increases* in human maladies, including depression, suicidality, and, as we have seen, in the mushrooming experience of loneliness.

Certainly, cultural attitudes have changed to produce such growth in isolation and loneliness, but what might be behind those cultural changes? One of the most likely candidates is technology, since it changes so drastically all manners of ways in which we live our lives.

In *Laudato Si'*, Pope Francis described and warned of a modern process of "rapidification," in which changes in work and technology, and the pressures that come with them, have accelerated more quickly than ever before, at a pace far outstripping "the naturally slow pace of biological evolution." In *Bowling Alone*, Robert Putnam provided some interesting evidence on the *pace* of the introduction of various technologically advanced consumer goods in the last century. Here are the statistics (abridged) at a glance:

The Pace of Introduction of Selected Consumer Goods [88]

Technological Invention	Household Penetration 1%	Years to Reach 75% of Households
Telephone	1890	67
Automobile	1908	52
Radio	1923	14
Television	1948	7

[88] Adapted from Putnam, *Bowling Alone*, p. 217, with some other inventions omitted.

So, television's expansion was remarkably rapid in the United States. Further, notable declines in civic and social engagement were noted within a decade of television's widespread availability. Studies showed that the more time people watched TV, the less they spent engaged with others, even with members of their own families, and the more televisions there were in a house, the more likely this was to be the case. Also, research indicates that increased television viewing was not just a *consequence* of less social engagement, but a powerful *cause* of decline in virtually every form of civic and social engagement. Per Putnam, the data suggests that for each additional hour of television watched per day, there was likely to be about a 10 percent reduction in forms of civic engagement, such as attending public meetings or writing to public officials. Although not all television viewing need be isolating, heavy viewing "is associated with lots of ... emotional difficulties" and, particular to our interests, "loneliness."[89]

Calling Pope Francis's concept of "rapidification" to mind, surely you can think of newer forms of technology that have revolutionized the workplace, the home, and human interactions more completely and rapidly than even television. *Bowling Alone* was published in 2000, and in its last pages Putnam predicted quite accurately that "no sector of American society will have more

---

[89] Putnam, *Bowling Alone*, 239.

influence on the future state of our social capital than the electronic mass media and especially the Internet."[90] Well, that future has arrived, and the electronic mass media is more massive and the Internet more interconnected than might even have been imagined at the start of the twenty-first century. In 2000, approximately one in two Americans used the Internet; by 2016, almost nine in ten did.[91] So what roles have technologies played in relation to loneliness?

Almost every time I have mentioned the subject of this book to friends and acquaintances, they have asked if I would be writing about the negative impact of cell phones in promoting loneliness. Phones contribute to reduced personal engagement when a phone call is substituted for a face-to-face visit. Over time, and especially with the younger generations, phone calls themselves have come to be seen as too anxiety-provoking and intrusive, only to be replaced by the yet more impersonal medium of texting. Gone are not only face-to-face interaction, but the familiarity and uniqueness of the human voice.

The impact of cell phones on loneliness has also been subjected to scientific research. A compelling modern study is clinical psychologist Sherry Turkle's *Alone Together: Why We Expect More from Technology and Less*

[90] Ibid., 410.

[91] Pew Research Center, *Internet Broadband Fact Sheet*, January 12, 2017, http://www.pewinternet.org/fact-sheet/internet-broadband/.

from Each Other. One of the many things she examines is the increased anxiety over face-to-face conversation and even telephone conversations among many young people today, leading them to send massive numbers of texts each day, and yet youths certainly have no monopoly on the use of cell phones to diminish attentive human interactions. She relates stories of the lonely teen, for example, who is picked up from school by her mother, only to be ignored the whole trip home by her mother, who remains absorbed in her phone.

Have you ever been speaking with a friend or family member only to be interrupted and ignored when that person answers the phone in his or her pocket? Have you ever been the one who answered and ignored someone? Have you ever called someone on the phone and heard the clicking of a keyboard in the background or pauses in conversation that suggest the person you are speaking to is multitasking while on the line?

As for another new form of technology, I was surprised by the findings in the entire first half of Dr. Turkle's *Alone Together*, although perhaps some readers with young children or grandchildren would not be surprised. I refer to the technological phenomenon of *robotics*. Dr. Turkle has done extensive research since the 1990s with children's electronic, robotic toys, from "digital pets" to simulated human babies. Sadly, some children come to prefer electronic pets to real ones, since, for example, they do not leave messes!

A new development in the care of the elderly involves the use of robots, from a seal-like pet selling in high volume from Japan to Denmark, to futuristic plans of humanoid robots to replace or supplement real human caretakers. Turkle tells of sociable robots being used in nursing homes, quoting one director who said, "Loneliness makes people sick. This could at least partially offset a vital factor that makes people sick."[92] Turkle then relates the tales of two men in their seventies who talk to and grow attached to robotic dolls. After a year, "both end up with My Real Baby as their closest companion." These two men are nearly the same age and live in the same hall. No mention is made of any companionship between them.

Perhaps most striking was Turkle's reporting of the practice in Japan, started in the 1990s, of busy adult children hiring actors to play them while visiting elderly parents in nursing homes! Turkle wondered, "If you are willing to send in an actor, why not send in a robot?"[93]

So here we are in 2017, surrounded by televisions, computers, cell phones, and perhaps soon by robots as well, while social and emotional isolation climb at alarming rates.

---

[92] Sherry Turkle, *Alone Together: Why We Expect More from Technology and Less from Each Other* (New York: Basic Books, 2011), 109.
[93] Ibid.

Conclusion

With You Always

Fear not, for I am with you, be not dismayed, for I
am your God: I will strengthen you, I will help you,
I will uphold you with my victorious right hand.

—Isaiah 41:10

Lo, I am with you always, to the close of the age.

—Matthew 28:20

Having Faced the Faces of Loneliness

We've faced many of the faces of loneliness in the pages of this book. Of course, loneliness itself has no face; what we've faced are the faces of *people* who feel lonely. Such a face might belong to a child who has been snubbed or bullied, who doesn't have a friend, or who has been left home alone too long, too often; to a teen who has moved into a new school, has experienced the divorce of her parents, and doesn't feel that she fits in; to a young adult away from home at college or in a new city starting a new job for the first time; to a middle-aged person whose spouse has declared that love will no longer keep them together, or who has retired early and only then finds out how much his coworkers really meant to him; to an elderly woman who has lost the mate of their youth after nearly a lifetime together, or who has left the family home for a nursing home, wondering when those she has nursed and cared for in their youth might find the time to drop by. Perhaps such a face looks back at you in the mirror.

Hopefully, though, we are now a little better equipped to face the faces of loneliness and see them more clearly through the trifocals of faith, hope, and charity. The lonely will no longer be invisible to us, and seeing them will remind us of our call to share our faith, hope, and loving charity with them, to play what role we might to bridge the emotional or social isolation they feel. We've seen how interventions for loneliness based on psychological research can include changing one's social thinking habits, improving one's social skills, and supplying social supports and connections of various kinds. We've seen how such changes in thinking, feeling, and acting take on newer and richer dimensions when practiced in light of the wisdom of the Church.

What comfort and guidance we receive from theologians and saints who show us how to embrace periods of solitude for our own and our neighbor's greater benefit, how God has provided us the most wonderful gift of spiritual friendship with our neighbor *through* Him, the loving friendship of charity directly *with* Him, so that we may all live our lives *in* Him.

Christ told us to love God first of all and our neighbors as ourselves, and we should not forget the part about ourselves. Although we should all be well aware of our own weakness and sinfulness, we should love ourselves to the extent that we realize we are worthy of striving to overcome them, so worthy that Christ gave His life so we could do so. We should love ourselves enough to embrace the struggle to be rid of loneliness or to bear it if we can't be completely free of it.

Also, we should never let either low self-esteem or a misguided sense of humility prevent us from reaching out to comfort and be there for another person who is lonely. We might ask ourselves, "Who cares if I should smile at someone, or say hello, or remember and call out their name, or strike up a conversation, or invite them to join me at Mass, at some other event, or to work on some project together?" That small gesture may make all the difference to some lonely person and might even bud into a true friendship we both will come to cherish. It is certain, however, that God will care, for He has commanded us to love each other, and He told us Himself: "You are my friends if you do what I command you" (John 15:14)

All the Lonely People: Where Do They All Come From?

Where do all the lonely people come from? They, or perhaps more precisely we, all come from God, of course, in whom every one of us "live and move and have our being" (Acts 17:28). Indeed, He knows and cares about each one of us individually: "Before I formed you in the womb I knew you" (Jer. 1:5), and as the psalmist declared: "For thou didst form my inward parts, thou didst knit me together in my mother's womb" (Ps. 139:13). What a wondrous thing that this Maker of us all, and of all that is, has also asked us to call Him "Our Father" (Matt. 6:9).

Perhaps the modern, secular notion that we are not from God, but live and move and exist merely through chance, has helped give rise to the epidemic of loneliness. As Catholics, we know that we are all sons and daughters of God. We know that every person has worth as a child of God and should not despair through loneliness. We know that we *can* do something about it through Christ, who strengthens us and who is with us always.

All the lonely people come from God, and God waits to welcome us back to Him in eternity, where Christ has prepared many mansions for us, and will be with us always as we look upon His face in the beatific vision. In the meantime, let's do our share to reach out to our lonely brothers and sisters in as many ways as we can to help make them feel more at home during our brief stay at this inn we call earth, so that they might share our eternal friendship should we reach our final destination in heaven.

About the Author

Kevin Vost

Kevin Vost (b. 1961) holds a Doctor of Psychology in Clinical Psychology (Psy.D.) degree from Adler University in Chicago. He has taught at Aquinas College in Nashville, the University of Illinois at Springfield, MacMurray College, and Lincoln Land Community College. He has served as a research review committee member for American Mensa, a society promoting the scientific study of human intelligence, and as an advisory board member for the International Association of Resistance Trainers, an organization that certifies personal fitness trainers. In 2017 Kevin and his wife, Kathy, became lay Dominican Associates with the Dominican Sisters of Springfield, Illinois.

Dr. Vost is the author of over a dozen Catholic books, has appeared on hundreds of Catholic radio and television broadcasts, and has traveled across the United States and Ireland, giving talks on the themes of his books. When home, he continues to drink great drafts of coffee while studying timeless, Thomistic tomes in the company of his wife, their two sons, and their two dogs.

Sophia Institute

Sophia Institute is a nonprofit institution that seeks to nurture the spiritual, moral, and cultural life of souls and to spread the Gospel of Christ in conformity with the authentic teachings of the Roman Catholic Church.

Sophia Institute Press fulfills this mission by offering translations, reprints, and new publications that afford readers a rich source of the enduring wisdom of mankind.

Sophia Institute also operates two popular online Catholic resources: CrisisMagazine.com and CatholicExchange.com.

Crisis Magazine provides insightful cultural analysis that arms readers with the arguments necessary for navigating the ideological and theological minefields of the day. Catholic Exchange provides world news from a Catholic perspective as well as daily devotionals and articles that will help you to grow in holiness and live a life consistent with the teachings of the Church.

In 2013, Sophia Institute launched Sophia Institute for Teachers to renew and rebuild Catholic culture through service to Catholic education. With the goal of nurturing the spiritual, moral, and cultural life of souls, and an abiding respect for the role and work of teachers, we strive to provide materials and programs that are at once enlightening to the mind and ennobling to the heart; faithful and complete, as well as useful and practical.

Sophia Institute gratefully recognizes the Solidarity Association for preserving and encouraging the growth of our apostolate over the course of many years. Without their generous and timely support, this book would not be in your hands.

www.SophiaInstitute.com
www.CatholicExchange.com
www.CrisisMagazine.com
www.SophiaInstituteforTeachers.org

Sophia Institute Press® is a registered trademark of Sophia Institute.
Sophia Institute is a tax-exempt institution as defined by the
Internal Revenue Code, Section 501(c)(3). Tax I.D. 22-2548708.